Devotions for a New Day

By Timothy D. Holder
& Jill Holder

All Scripture quotations are from the Christian Standard Bible®. Copyright © 2017 by Holman Bible Publishers. Used by permission.

Christian Standard Bible®, and CSB® are federally registered trademarks of Holman Bible Publishers.

All rights reserved © 2021

TDH Communications
Knoxville, TN 2021

ISBN 9798496814225

Acknowledgements

from Tim

I am thankful for all the people who allowed me to invoke their names in my stories. My life is so much richer because of my friends and family. They are a blessing to me that I do not take for granted.

I am also thankful for the talent of Josh Martin, who provided the front cover art and took the photo on the back cover. You can see more of his great work online by following him on Instagram @longwalkphotos.

This book was made better by the guest devotional from Elissa Keck Hodge. She is a friend who is always good to work with. Things tend to go better when Elissa is involved with them.

Jill Holder contributed to this project in several ways. She developed a vision for the cover, helped significantly with the title, and wrote many of the devotions. She inspired several of my devotions by being such a significant and special part of my life. The work I did on this book was easier because of Jill's encouragement. I find it is also easier to work when I am happy. Being with Jill has made me very happy. I am blessed indeed.

I am humbled by the Lord's great mercy and blessing. And I am so grateful.

from Jill

If I could go back in time and give a sentence of insight to my eighteen-year-old self, I would say, "The path is not going to be what you are hoping, but it will be better than that." Life is a journey of twists and turns intermingled with beautiful moments, and I am grateful to all the friends, family, teachers, and mentors that have encouraged me and made a difference in my life along the way.

I am thankful to my parents, Jim and Joyce Jackson, and to my grandmothers, Nora Jackson and Elizabeth Johnson, for instilling a love for Jesus in me as a child. They took me to church, taught me scripture and life lessons, and loved me. I am eternally grateful.

Five of life's most beautiful joys are my children, and I am thankful for them. Jessica, Jonathan, Joshua, Jackson, and Joseph are precious to me, and it is an honor and a privilege to be their mom. Through teaching them, they have taught me as well. They each have a piece of my heart with them wherever they go.

My gratitude to my husband, Tim, goes beyond even what words can express. His love, encouragement, and support in my life help me to grow and become a better woman. I am thankful for that and for the joy that we share each day!

Last, but certainly not least, I am thankful to the Lord for His presence and guidance throughout my life. Every day with Him really is "a new day"!

Table of Contents

1. Audacity, Mark 16:15-16
2. Consequences, Romans 6:23
3. Gratitude, Psalm 103:1-2
4. Daisy-Chains, Genesis 12:1
5. Overwhelmed, Philippians 4:13
6. Perspective, Colossians 3:1-2
7. Anger, Ephesians 4:26
8. Tact, Proverbs 16:24
9. Winter, Lamentations 3:22-23
10. Movement, Colossians 3:23
11. Misconceptions, Ezekiel 40:10
12. Witnessing, Matthew 9:38
13. Sacrifice, Luke 2:19
14. Truth, Psalm 119:9
15. Memories, 1 Peter 5:7
16. Focus, Matthew 5:16
17. Hobson's Choice, Proverbs 25:25
18. Boldness, 2 Timothy 1:7
19. The Word, 2 Timothy 3:14-16
20. Cynicism, 2 Corinthians 5:17
21. Grit, Luke 21:19
22. Choices, Proverbs 12:15
23. Bravery, 2 Chronicles 20:15-17
24. Communication, 1 Corinthians 14:9
25. Holiness, 1 Peter 1:15
26. Faith, Hebrews 11:1
27. Encouragement, 1 Chronicles 28:20
28. More, 2 Corinthians 9:8
29. Direction, Proverbs 3:5-6
30. Discipleship, Luke 9:23
31. Selfishness, Philippians 2:4
32. Pride, Proverbs 16:18
33. Instructions, Proverbs 8:33
34. Holiness, 1 Peter 1:16

35. Companionship, Ecclesiastes 4:12
36. Discernment, Acts 17:11
37. Communication, Proverbs 25:11
38. Humor, Ecclesiastes 3:4A
39. His Presence, Isaiah 41:10
40. Pride, Isaiah 2:12
41. Imitations, Psalm 16:11
42. Action, 1 Peter 1:13
43. Heroes, Galatians 6:9
44. Integrity, Proverbs 28:6
45. Perceptions, Hebrews 3:1
46. Devotion for a New Day, Psalm 118:24
47. Wise Counsel, Ephesians 4:25
48. Mystery, 1 Corinthians 13:12
49. Effort, Colossians 3:23
50. Secrets, 1 John 3:3
51. Planning, Matthew 5:6
52. Lessons, Proverbs 16:16
53. Sacrifice and Celebration, Mark 10:45
54. Consistency, Matthew 6:24
55. Temptations, 1 Corinthians 6:18
56. Persistence, James 1:12
57. God's Will, Jeremiah 33:3
58. Shortcuts, Matthew 16:24
59. Role Modeling, Matthew 18:6
60. Friends, Proverbs 13:20
61. Animals, Job 1:8
62. Illusion, James 5:16
63. Unity, Philippians 2:2
64. Goals, Psalm 127:1
65. Discernment, Philippians 1:9-11
66. Change, Ecclesiastes 3:11A
67. Repetition, Galatians 6:14-15
68. Blessings, Psalm 103:2
69. Priorities, Colossians 3:2
70. Surprises, James 1:3

71. Titles, Acts 11:26C
72. Feelings, Galatians 5:22-23
73. God's Love, Ephesians 2:4-5
74. Excuses, John 15:22
75. Discipline, Colossians 2:18
76. Service, 1 Corinthians 12:5-6
77. Words, John 14:6
78. Principles, Matthew 6:33
79. Everyday Miracles, Luke 12:7
80. The Beginning, Psalm 30:5B

Day 1

Audacity

by Timothy D. Holder

Mark 16:15-16 "Then He said to them, 'Go into all the world and preach the Gospel to all creation. Whoever believes and is baptized will be saved, but whoever does not believe will be condemned.'"

I walked into a fast food restaurant and went up to the counter. "Can I get a bottled water?" I asked.

"Sure," the cashier replied. "Would you like to add a McRib Sandwich to that order?"

Maybe it's just me, but that seemed like a rather…inorganic add-on sale.

I posted the encounter on social media, of course, because weird exchanges with cashiers are apparently a thing with me.[1] A guy I knew from college responded to the post by saying, "She's sales royalty; bow slightly as you hand her the keys to your car."

Maybe he was onto something. I mean, I was not ordering the McRib, so what did she have to lose? It was not like I was going to say, "How dare you ask me that?! Okay, forget it! Now I don't want the water either!"

She had nothing to lose and everything to gain. Maybe she was a little over the top, but could we learn something from this? Maybe we could use just a little of that cashier's gumption when it comes to sharing our faith.

---

[1] See *Devotions for the Day* for examples of this strange reality that is my life.

Let us pray for some audacity today when it comes to communicating our faith to those who need to hear about it.

Day 2

Consequences

by Timothy D. Holder

Romans 6:23 "For the wages of sin is death, but the gift of God is eternal life in Christ Jesus our Lord."

Email can be a wonderful thing. For example, I was quite pleased when I received an email notification from Amazon regarding a purchase I did *not* make. I was notified that a digital copy of *Barbie as the Island Princess* had been charged to my account.

Imagine my surprise!

For the record: I did not buy it. In fact, I had just gotten home from eating dinner at a restaurant with someone. She could verify my story if we were still on speaking terms (which is a story for another time. And by "another time" I mean "never").

Anyway, the movie only cost me four dollars and change, but I still contacted Amazon and had it removed as a matter of principle.

Amazon was super nice about deducting the charge, and that was the end of the matter…except for the Barbie-themed recommendations that popped up for a while after that, based on "my purchasing history." You might not realize this, but Barbie has had a prolific career in the digital movie industry.

I do not believe that someone hacked my account merely to order an inexpensive kids' movie, starring a doll. I think it was an honest mistake by the company, but there were still consequences. I was mildly inconvenienced, and Amazon was out four bucks and change because someone somewhere did something that should not have been done.

There are times, though, when the consequences of actions are much more extreme. For example, some of us might be facing a temptation that seems irresistible. We would do well to remember that other people are impacted by our choices. Let us pray for the character to not make selfish decisions that will hurt those close to us.

Day 3

Gratitude

by Jill Holder

Psalm 103:1-2 "My soul, bless the Lord, and all that is within me, bless His holy name. My soul, bless the Lord, and do not forget all His benefits."

It had been a rough year. Not just a downturn in life, but one of those crazy hard years that threatens to knock the breath out of you. As the year was drawing to an end, I knew that God had been faithful and present, but I was still feeling a bit weary. My Scripture reading that day dealt with being thankful for the many blessings that God brings to our lives, and as I read, I began to realize that I had been so consumed with dealing with the difficulties that I had lost sight of the daily blessings that God had brought my way. I recalled the "big" things, but the daily miracles escaped me.

It was December 31st, and while New Year's resolutions have never been my habit because that date is also my birthday, I knew that this year I needed a change. So, I went to the store and bought a pretty floral calendar, placed it on my bedside table, and resolved to not go to sleep at night until I had jotted down at least one thing that day that I was thankful for, something special that God had brought about in that particular twenty-four-hour period. I entitled the calendar "My Thankful Journal," and as the new year began, so did a new phase of my journey.

At first, simple words like "sleep," "progress," and "clarity" were written in the daily squares. But as the days and weeks passed, I found that the spaces were becoming more and more full of words. After a month, I was writing in tiny print to try and fit all the blessings in each day's space, sometimes spilling over into the margins. I came to realize that focusing on the many good things that God was bringing to my daily life wasn't just changing my awareness of Him, but my attitude was changing as well. I began waking up in excited anticipation of the wonderful things that God was going to do that day. The morning sunlight seemed brighter, my children's laughter seemed to come more frequently, and relationships with family and friends seemed dearer and more fulfilling. The gifts had been there all the time, but now that my focus was on the correct perspective, they were more clearly visible, and my attitude was greatly improved as well.

  At the end of the year, I took some time to look back over the many ways that God was present in my life. It was overwhelming to see how He had walked with me and provided for me every step of the way. So, I bought a new calendar and kept on going! It has been multiple years since I started these Thankful Journals, and they are a testament to how much we have to be thankful for and how consistently God walks with us through our daily lives, caring for us in big ways and small ways because of His great love for us! Let us pray today for a spirit of gratitude.

Day 4

Daisy-Chains

by Timothy D. Holder

Genesis 12:1 "The Lord said to Abram: Go from your land, your relatives, and your father's house to the land that I will show you."

Jill and I first met in person at a restaurant on a Friday night. She was late because she went to the wrong restaurant and sat there for a bit before realizing her error. Fortunately, I had a book to read and the patience of a saint.

Really, she was not that late at all. In fact, I just assumed she was running a few minutes behind. I had no idea she had time to go to a different restaurant, realize her mistake, and then join me.

I did not know on our first date that we would end up as a couple, but I did assume I would have a pleasant time. We had spent several days texting and talking before the first date. I knew she was a believer, smart, interesting, and pretty. I figured that even if we decided not to date, we would at least have a pleasant evening.

But we did start dating. When I learned that she liked to teach and write, and she showed me some things she had written, I asked her to write something for this book. Then I asked her to write a lot for this book. As you can tell by the names on the book cover, things continued to escalate.

"Daisy-chaining" is a term I learned from a former boss. It basically refers to how we can string one thing to another to another. In our lives, it is interesting how God can move us from Point A to Point B to Point C to Point D.

There are times when we are standing at Point A and have no idea that Point D is awaiting us. It is too far from where we currently are. We would do well to trust the Lord to guide our circumstances when we cannot see the way.

I am experiencing certain blessings in my life specifically because of Jill. I did not anticipate all these things when I first began to date her. But this idea does not just apply to romantic relationships. We would do well to not assume that we have our journey figured out. When it comes to our careers, our family and friend relationships, and our opportunities, we do not know what connections the Lord will lead us to or what curves there will be in our road. Let us pray today for open eyes and a sense of wonder as we wait and see where and how the Lord might lead us.

Day 5

Overwhelmed

by Timothy D. Holder

Philippians 4:13 "I am able to do all things through Him who strengthens me."

Many years ago, when I was a younger, pluckier version of the man I am today, I had a goal: I wanted to make more money. The Christian bookstore I worked at was not paying a lot, so I was trying to figure out what I could do to improve my economic situation. One day, someone I knew said something about security guards who got paid to sit through their shifts, just reading books or whatever. I thought, *Man, they get paid to read? That's awesome.*

I promptly applied for a job with a security company.

They hired me and gave me my first assignment. They stressed that I was not to show up with a book as they were not paying me to read.

Clearly, I had applied for work with the wrong security company.

I showed up for my first assignment, which was at an office park on a Friday night. My supervisor, Captain Jones, started off my briefing by asking if I had brought a book because it would *probably* be a slow night.

I could stop right here, and this story would be the perfect summary of how my life goes, but there's more.

Captain Jones explained that I needed to patrol the parking lot periodically through the night to keep an eye on the office buildings. Vandals had broken in during the last weekend. They had made their way into the buildings, but they had trouble breaking into the individual offices because the interior doors were made of reinforced steel. These particular vandals, however, were quite committed to their work. They simply chopped through the walls with hatchets and then trashed some of the offices.

Yes, you read that correctly, dear reader. The vandals—you know, the people that I am supposed to keep an eye out for—had hatchets. I had been encouraged to bring a heavy flashlight, and with that I was supposed to protect the buildings from a gang with hatchets.

I guess taking a flashlight to a hatchet fight is not exactly the same thing as taking a knife to a gunfight, but I still felt that I was at a tactical disadvantage.

Captain Jones was not finished. The businesses were also concerned about a homeless guy who was living by a pond located near the parking lot. They had tried to confront him during the day, but they only found his chair and mattress. The plan was for me to cut my way through the brush in the dark and confront this homeless person and make him leave.

A better man might have been concerned with where the homeless man should go.

I was not a better man.

I was preoccupied with reviewing the percentages for homeless men and mental illness, and I was wondering how such a person might respond to being awakened by a stranger at his secluded camp in the dark.

As Captain Jones finished sharing with me the details of not one but two life-threatening scenarios, I was deciding that there were better ways to earn four dollars an hour.

My first night as a security guard turned out to be my last night as a security guard. There are times when life throws too much at us, and the best thing to do is just meet our most basic obligation and then walk away.

But sometimes in life we cannot simply walk away. Some situations must be endured until the end. Fortunately, we have help. Paul did not succeed in everything he attempted, but God got him through it all. He was able to endure difficult circumstances with God's help. And God still offers that same kind of help. Let us ask for His help to endure our trials today.

Day 6

Perspective

by Jill Holder

Colossians 3:1-2 "So if you have been raised with Christ, seek the things above, where Christ is, seated at the right hand of God. Set your minds on things above, not on earthly things."

One of my fondest memories as a little girl was riding on my daddy's shoulders! We had a frequent ritual when he came home from work. He would hold out his right hand, and I would grab two of his fingers in each of my little hands. We would count to three together, I would jump, and he would lift me through the air to land solidly on his shoulders. From my seat high above, as opposed to my usual viewpoint when I walked, everything took on a different perspective because I could see so much more.

One evening when I was a small child, my parents took me with them to a University of Tennessee basketball game. As we waited for the arena doors to open in the very crowded lobby of the Stokely Athletic Center, all I could see were the legs of other people pushing around me. It was hot and stuffy, and I thought we were stuck with no way out in any direction. But then my dad lifted me up onto his shoulders and my perspective changed. The air was fresh above the crowd. I could look ahead and see the big orange doors that we were going to go through and look behind to the glass doors where we had already been.

On a much larger scale, God wants us to have a heavenly perspective above our current circumstances. It is so easy to be consumed with the things of our lives that we can't see above where we are, and the past and future can become a blur as the overwhelming demands, burdens, and goals of today consume our mindsets. I recently saw an illustration of this fallacy of thinking. Imagine an immense coil of rope with only the very tip of one end dipped in red paint. The red tip represents our lives on earth, and the huge coiled section represents our remaining time in eternity with the exception that the coil would have no end. Why are we so consumed with the tip when eternity is so much greater?

So, how do we maintain a heavenly perspective? How do we view life from God's vantage point instead of becoming mired down in the situations of today? We need to spend time reading God's words to align our thoughts with His thoughts. Our, behavior, language, and thoughts usually become similar to those with whom we spend the most time, so if we want to act, talk, and think like God with a heavenly perspective, we have to spend time with Him. Often, in light of eternity, our problems on earth can seem less overwhelming and we find direction on how we use our time, influence, and resources.

Let us pray for a heavenly perspective on whatever situations arise today.

Day 7

Anger

by Timothy D. Holder

Ephesians 4:26 "Be angry and do not sin. Don't let the sun go down on your anger."

I was driving west on Interstate 40 early on a Sunday morning. I was supposed to pick up Jill so we could go to church. All of a sudden, all five lanes of traffic going my way slowed down. That was a little weird; usually when there is a traffic issue, one or two lanes will slow down first. It was one of those things where we crawled along for a while, then the traffic picked up speed, but there was no evidence of road construction or an accident.

For me, I occasionally get a little frustrated when I am stuck in traffic, but then if I see that the jam was caused by an accident, I will think *Okay, that person is having a harder time than me*, and it puts my problems in perspective. But without that experience, the frustration just grows unchecked. As this particular traffic jam dragged on, the cushion of time I had given myself expired, and now the opportunity to pick Jill up was out the window—we would just have to meet at the church.

As it was starting to look like I might be late, even with just driving straight to the church, the traffic finally picked up speed. It was at that point I realized I was stuck behind a big truck that could only do thirty-five miles an hour on the interstate. On the one hand, it was better than the five-to-ten miles an hour I had been doing, but on the other, it would still make me late for church.

I was in the third lane from the left, and I moved to the fourth lane because that was where the only opening was. I was not necessarily trying to pass the big slow truck, but as I accelerated up to the speed limit, that was the result.

I decided I would move back to the third lane because the driver in front of me was not exactly being Type A about getting to his destination. I looked behind me and to the side. The third lane was open, so I began to migrate over. As I made my move, I saw a red car in the second lane that was quickly closing in. I was in front of it, and there was room to spare between it and the slow-moving truck.

Now, I realize that based on my description, it might sound like I was passing on the right and weaving in and out of traffic, but really, I was just trying to get up to the speed limit. The driver of the red car, however, truly was weaving and speeding. And he got mad at me because I had inadvertently blocked him from continuing to speed as much as he wanted. He got on my tail and flashed his lights at me longer than I have ever been flashed in my life. Then after a pause he flashed me again, while still riding my tail. He carried on long enough that I briefly wondered if he was driving an unmarked police car and wanted to pull me over.

As we continued down the interstate, we passed three actual police cars located on the right shoulder of the road. Seeing them caused the driver behind me to calm down. He changed lanes and went about his business. I kept an eye on him, silently wishing he was going to the same place I was, just because that would have been super funny to me to give him a cheerful hello in the church parking lot.

If you drive long enough, you end up making mistakes, and I have certainly made my share. But for that day, my conscience was clear. I did not cut that driver off, nor was I in any way reckless. He was frustrated because of the traffic, and that put him on a short fuse with me.

I cannot help but wonder, though, how often we are like the driver from the second lane. Do we get mad about something going on in our lives and then take it out on other people? It is in times like these—when life is particularly difficult—that our witness can truly shine. It is in times like these that we can show the world something truly different.

Let us pray today that God will help us shine the light of His love and grace, even in the midst of frustrating circumstances.

Day 8

Tact

by Timothy D. Holder

Proverbs 16:24 "Pleasant words are a honeycomb: sweet to the taste and health to the body."

"Those who can, do. Those who can't, teach."
That is an old saying. I heard it years ago, and I read it again yesterday on Twitter. It is a saying I have thought about a lot over the years, especially since I have devoted more than half my life to teaching.

As an educator, let me say that I understand, I think, what this idea might be rooted in. Let me illustrate with a personal anecdote. For a year and a half, I studied Shaolin Kempo, which is a mixture of Kung Fu, Karate, and Jiu Jitsu. I loved it! But the more complicated moves did not come easily to me. After I had been practicing for the better part of a year, and as I was working on a series of moves that I was struggling to master, it struck me that I might be able to teach this martial art one day. Because I had to really break down and think through each move, I reasoned, I would be able to explain it in detail to someone else. If it had been effortless for me, I might have struggled to explain it to someone who did not grasp it so easily.

I enjoyed it, but I would probably never be amazing at it. That said, I believed I could master the technical side of it.

My point is that I think there is some validity to the notion that there are times and places where it would be accurate to say, "Those who can, do. Those who can't teach." It isn't always true, but it also isn't always, um, not true.

I like another saying: Read the room. Sometimes we should be able to comprehend what we should not say in front of a certain group.

One year when I was teaching at a private school, all the teachers from kindergarten through twelfth grade were meeting. The school had hired a new principal, and after hearing him speak, I was thankful he did not work with my group. He stood in front of an auditorium full of teachers, talked about how he never imagined himself working at a school, and said, "Because you know what they say, right? 'Those who can, do, and those who can't, teach.'"

There was no polite laughter at his attempt at humor; there was only shock and irritation. Even though, as I stated above, there is a context for that quotation, we did not want to hear it that morning. A whole bunch of woefully underpaid teachers, many of whom were feeling a little overwhelmed by thoughts of the end of summer and a full year of school ahead, did not appreciate being condescended to by a stranger whose message was "Wow, I thought I could do better than this."

Sometimes the words of others hurt us, and there are times when our words hurt other people. Let us pray today that God will give us the sensitivity and character to take a breath before we speak and then communicate with tact.

Day 9

Winter

by Jill Holder

Lamentations 3:22–23 "Because of the Lord's faithful love we do not perish, for His mercies never end. They are new every morning; great is Your faithfulness!"

The frost came last night, as I knew it would, and took my flowers away. A few random ones made it, but most turned brown and wilted during the night. I think this is why I've come to dread the late autumn every year. Flowers either die or lie dormant in their roots underground for months, and I miss them. I like the joy and the beauty that they bring to the world, growing, blooming, and spreading happiness just by being. The frost made me sad as it does every year.

And then I saw the ivy, each leaf fringed in lacy, white frost. Such unexpected beauty! While it was once merely a backdrop for the more vibrant blooms, hardly even noticed, in this season it was now the most beautiful plant in the garden.

The ivy was a reminder to me that God brings beauty and miracles in every season of life. In the spring and summer seasons, when all is going well and everything is happiness and joy, I see the miracles easily, and they bring me peace. But it is in the darker seasons of life where God reminds me of the miracles and gifts that have gone unnoticed. In these seasons, He teaches me to see deeper, to cherish more, to listen closer to His voice. This is where I'm taught trust and patience; this is where my faith grows most as I see that there are miracles all around me, even on the darker days. The peace here, while more difficult to obtain, is much deeper. The lessons learned are bigger. My foundation and character are formed during these times.

And I cherish the spring even more because I have lived through the winter.

Let us pray that we will seek the Lord's voice in all seasons of life.

Day 10

Movement

by Timothy D. Holder

Colossians 3:23 "Whatever you do, do it from the heart, as something done for the Lord and not for people."

My first full-time job was at a Christian bookstore shortly after I graduated college. It paid fifteen cents above minimum wage, which was $3.35 an hour at the time, and I worked there for about ten months. I bounced around with a few short-term jobs, then went back to the bookstore. They were at their quota for full time employees at that point, though, so my situation was a little worse than it was before. I was not exactly making full use of my private school college degree.

After another year spent spinning my wheels, I went back to college to get an education major. This was followed by a year of substitute teaching. The whole time, I was continuing to work part-time at the bookstore.

I got promoted to assistant manager and held that position for a year and a half before finally landing a job as a high school history teacher.

I enjoyed being at the Christian high school, but it paid so poorly that I needed to go back yet again to working part-time at the bookstore to make ends meet.

It was at this point that a guy I knew in college entered the story. He had been a year behind me in school, and after graduation he quickly worked his way up in a Christian organization. He saw me stocking books on a shelf at the store one night, and he expressed surprise that I was working there. He asked if I was the manager, and I said I was not.

I could tell he was surprised that I was "just" a bookstore employee, given how many years earlier I had graduated from school. I could have explained that I was a schoolteacher and this was just my side job, but I didn't. Partially, it was because I did not know this guy that well, so I was not too concerned with how he was clearly judging me.

Paradoxically, though, I think there might have been a part of me that felt like I deserved to be judged. I had spent years at the bookstore without seriously moving up (except temporarily) and growing much as an employee. I was glad I was teaching high school, but it had taken me a while to figure out what to do with myself. From middle school through college, I had a plan for my life. I never felt concerned or confused during those years about my career track. I had it all figured out.

And then I did not.

My experiences were all valuable in shaping me into the man I would become, but I was a little slow, perhaps, in getting on the path God had for me. Or maybe the timing was perfect, but I had definitely needed to move forward when I finally did.

Is that where you are right now? Maybe you have taken your foot off the gas when it comes to a ministry you were involved in or pursuing. Maybe you have fallen out of the habit of something as basic as attending church. Maybe you have hit the pause button on your career or a relationship.

Is it time to go forward? Is it time to change direction?

Move!

Pray for guidance, pray for gumption, and move.

Day 11

Misconceptions

by Timothy D. Holder

Ezekiel 40:10 "There were three recesses on each side of the east gate, each with the same measurements, and the jambs on either side also had the same measurements."

One of my favorite college professors only taught part-time at my school, and I believe he was in the Christian Ministries Department. I was a Bible major, so I only had one class with him, but I loved it and him because I heard him teach (and preach once in chapel) with great enthusiasm and humor.

Alas, one of my most vivid memories of him is the time I embarrassed myself in his class. He asked one day if every verse of the Bible is of equal importance. I was not typically a student who blurted out answers, but that day I did.

"Well, of course," I said with both immediacy and confidence.

Almost simultaneously, three other students replied with various versions of "absolutely not."

Thankfully, he focused on the three who were correct, thus allowing me to process my humiliation without being the focus of the class.

I had thought my reasoning was sound: If the Bible was God's Word, wasn't it all equally important?

Well, certainly God can touch us through any part of His Word, but that does not make each verse equally important. Let me put it this way: If you only had time to share one verse with someone who did not know Jesus, would you share something like John 3:16 or the verse from Ezekiel cited above?

The point of this devotion is not actually related to the inspiration of Scripture. It's that sometimes we believe stuff because it just makes sense to us, but it really does not stand up to God-given logical thinking. It is not uncommon for some of us to do this with beliefs we might have inherited from our family or friend group instead of from Scripture.

May we today prayerfully examine our beliefs and see if we are holding onto prejudices or other illogical views that hamper our communication of the Gospel.

Day 12

Witnessing

by Timothy D. Holder

Matthew 9:38 "Therefore, pray to the Lord of the harvest to send out workers into His harvest."

When I was in my early thirties, I decided to join the Reserves. I will not reveal which branch of the Armed Forces I tried to join, because I am about to paint a picture that is not flattering, and I have a lot of respect for the military. I don't want to cast on unfavorable light on a specific branch of service just because one man was having a bad day.

I wanted to join the Reserves because I wanted to serve my country; the orderliness, discipline, and clear-cut chain of command appealed to me; and, frankly, I was a graduate student who was teaching college part-time and I needed a little more income each month.

When I walked into the recruiter's office, he was sitting at his desk and talking on the phone. He said, "The (name of service) has already cost me two marriages, and if you can't get me to Chicago, it's going to cost me a third!"

At that point, two thoughts entered my mind: One, he was clearly having a bad day. Two, he was probably not going to win any awards for recruiting.

He eventually got off the phone and asked me what I wanted. I thought that would be rather obvious since he was a recruiter in a recruiting office that was open for the sole purpose of recruitment, but instead of pointing that out, I simply said I was interested in joining the Reserves as an officer.

He asked if I thought I was too good to serve as an enlisted man. I replied that my father had been an enlisted man for twenty years, and I was proud of that. But, I said, I had spent a lot of time and money on my education, and I wanted to do things where I would get credit for that. Otherwise, I would have made a rather poor investment.

The recruiter decided that my rationale made sense, and he tried to work with me. Ultimately, this was a door that did not open, given my age and credentials (if I had been a lawyer or a dentist, things would have turned out differently).

I think about this recruiter occasionally, though, because he really did not put his best foot forward with me. He had something going on in his life that overshadowed the work he was doing for the military.

What about us? Are we committed to sharing our faith, or do other things—big and small—distract us from the work of sharing the Gospel? Let us pray today that we would be locked in on sharing the love of Christ with someone.

Day 13

Sacrifice

by Jill Holder

Luke 2:19 "But Mary was treasuring up all these things in her heart and meditating on them."

Every Christmas Eve after attending the candlelight service at church, our family comes home and reads the true story from the Bible about the birth of Christ. We pass the big Bible around and read a few verses each. Through the years, we have changed from only a parent reading the words to each child taking a turn as he or she learned to read, allowing everyone to experience the sweet time of taking their first turn to hold the Bible and read the words aloud. And each year, Luke 2:19 tugs at me. It is one of my favorite Scriptures.

My oldest son was born in September, and Christmas seemed to come so quickly that year in my haze from lack of sleep, taking care of both a new baby and a busy three-year-old daughter, and keeping up with all the church and preschool activities. We made it to the Christmas musical that year, and I continued my break from singing in the choir to sit in the congregation with my little girl and hold my newborn son in my arms. As a beautiful soloist portrayed Mary holding baby Jesus, I looked down at my own precious baby boy and wondered how Mary could have felt. It hit me deeply that night; as Mary pondered all the events surrounding the birth of Jesus, had she realized who He was and what His future would be?

Certainly, all my life I have been taught about the sacrifice that God had made in sending His own son to die as a sacrifice for our sins (John 3:16), but I had mostly thought of the sacrifice from the viewpoint of the one who benefitted from the gift rather than the Giver. I could not fathom sacrificing my own son, even if it meant saving the entire universe! And that night I realized more fully how much God must love each of us if He was willing to send Jesus to earth to endure the horrible pain of the cross for us. If I was the only sinner, He would have sent His Son for me. If you were the only sinner, He would have sent Jesus to pay the price for you!

And so, I gained a greater appreciation for what Mary must have eventually known she would sacrifice and a deeper love for God's gift of salvation for my children. Save me, and I am eternally grateful. The gift of salvation for my children, sacrificing His own for mine, is the greatest gift He could have ever given me. If He has sacrificed so very much for us, can we not live for Him? Let us pray today to deepen our understanding of God's precious gift of His Son to us.

Day 14

Truth

by Timothy D. Holder

Psalm 119:9 "How can a young man keep his way pure? By keeping Your Word."

James Madison, who would later become the fourth President of the United States, was an excellent student. He was so studious, in fact, that after graduating from college, he stayed at school an extra year so he could study even more. One of his areas of interest was Hebrew, which he wanted to learn so he could read the Old Testament in the original language.

I wish I could tell you that he wanted to do this because he was so devout in his Christian faith, but I cannot. The story of his faith is rather murky, and many historians would argue against the idea that he was an orthodox Christian.

Whatever the ultimate destination of his soul (and for the record, it is possible that he was a believer), his motivation for reading the Old Testament in Hebrew is easier to discern: He wanted to gain insight into how to set up a new government from scratch.

The point is that Madison saw the Bible as a source from which he could gain knowledge. God's Word explains the means by which we may be saved, but it also provides wisdom for how to strengthen marriages, maintain sexual purity, not become a slave to alcohol, be ethical in the workplace, and (for Madison) how to set up a government for a new nation.

For those of us who have neglected our Bible reading or have failed to ask God to change us through His

Word, let us prayerfully submit to God's written truths today.

Day 15

Memories

by Timothy D. Holder

1 Peter 5:7 "Casting all your cares on Him, because He cares about you."

Eric Davis was a Major League Baseball player who spent many years with the Cincinnati Reds, a little time with my beloved St. Louis Cardinals, and a few years with some other teams too. I have thought of him a few times since he broke into the big leagues in the 1980s. What fascinated me about him was he hit a lot of home runs (in his best season he had 37), but he was not a big, strong guy. He was actually much more of a thin, fast player. His best season as a base stealer saw him swipe 80.

So, how did a player built like that hit so many home runs? He used a really skinny bat. It allowed him to generate a lot of speed when the wood hit the ball. The tradeoff was that using such a thin piece of lumber made it harder to make contact with the ball. Sure, he stole a lot of bases, and he hit a bunch of home runs, but then he hit, like, .207 (which is pretty terrible).

The point of this devotion was going to be focused on the importance of shrewdness. We Christians are involved in work where the results matter, and Eric Davis got results by trying something unconventional. We need to advance on many fronts to do the work of the Kingdom of God. That means we need to do unconventional things as well as conventional ones.

There is only one problem with my beautifully crafted and insightful devotion: My story is not accurate. I looked up Mr. Davis' stats, and in the year I was thinking of, my dude hit .293. His career average was .269, which is somewhere south of awesome, but for a long career that features some decline at the end, which is typical of Major Leaguers who are good enough to stick around for many years, what he did was not too shabby at all.

But, of course, that did leave me with a quandary: What was I going to do with this devotion? An interesting thing for me to consider was the unreliability of memory. As I said above, I have thought about this guy over the years, his creative approach to batting, and the pros and cons thereof. But I was remembering it wrongly.

It begs the question: How many hurts and frustrations have we held onto that are actually just situations that we remember wrongly or misperceived in the first place? Maybe you thought a group of people were laughing at you, but they were really laughing at something else. Perhaps I thought a boss was treating me unfairly, but maybe she always handled her business the same with everybody.

There are two important things to note here. One, many of our past hurts are real. Two, our number one reason for letting go of past hurts is that Jesus loves us and calls us to forgive others as He has forgiven us.

All of that said, my point here still stands. Some of us rehearse and retell stories about life not being fair and/or someone saying or doing something that hurt our feelings. How many of those events are just...remembered wrongly?

Let us make an effort today to let it go. God has graced us with today. Let us ask the Lord to help us to not let pain from yesterday ruin our today.

Day 16

Focus

by Jill Holder

Matthew 5:16 "In the same way, let your light shine before others, so that they may see your good works and give glory to your Father in heaven."

An acquaintance of mine years ago shared a personal experience that happened at the end of his senior year of high school. He attended a large public school. On the last day of his senior year, the yearbooks were passed out and several hours were set aside for autographing each other's pages. As he walked around, writing notes in his friends' yearbooks, he left his own book on a table and came back to find it later.

After graduation, he sat and read the personal notes that his friends had written and was surprised to find an inscription by a fellow student that he barely knew. Although they had attended school together for twelve years, he couldn't recall a single conversation they had shared. In fact, he did not recollect even passing comments in the hallway between classes. This classmate had written to him that he had been watching him for all those years. He had heard him speak of God, church, and his youth group. As he listened to his speech and watched his actions, he wrote, he had come to realize that something was missing in his own life. Although his family was not into worshipping or believing in God, he had chosen to give his life to Christ because of the example he had seen.

No matter where we are or what we are doing, others are watching us. We are always setting an example, whether good or bad. I have had a note attached to my dresser mirror for several years that reminds me to live a life that exemplifies what I hope others will strive to become. The people we are reaching with our actions may be our coworkers. They may be our family members. But people that we do not even know are watching us, too. How can we let our light shine to draw others to God? According to the Bible, this is accomplished by not conforming to the world we live in but by the *renewing of our minds*. That renewing happens when we focus on God through prayer, read the Bible, see Scripture on our walls, and peruse the daily verse that pops up on our cell phone screens. We are renewed through the teaching in church and especially when worshipping Him!

    Let us focus today on worshipping Him and letting His light shine through us.

Day 17

Hobson's Choice

by Timothy D. Holder

Proverbs 25:25 "Good news from a distant land is like cold water to a parched throat."

For years, I have known *Hobson's Choice* was an old movie. What I did not know is that "Hobson's Choice" is also an old expression that has a cool backstory.

Apparently, many years ago there was a man who rented out his horses (back when that was a main source of transportation). People always wanted to rent the best of his herd, but that meant those animals tended to get worn down. The man, Mr. Hobson, decided to protect the health of his best horses by putting his entire stock on a rotation. When a customer showed up, he or she could rent the next horse in the lineup, or they could walk to their next destination. Technically, the customer had a choice, but it was not much of one. This dilemma of being offered a choice when only one of the options was practical became known as a "Hobson's Choice."

Do we present the Gospel in those terms? "Hey, don't you want to accept Jesus? If you don't, then you'll burn in hell." The Gospel is good news. It is a love story that offers hope. Do we share it that way? Do we see it that way when it comes to our own salvation?

The Gospel is more than a Hobson's Choice. It is a plan created by the Maker of the universe to save us.

Let us today pray that we can share the Gospel without scare tactics.

Day 18

Boldness

by Timothy D. Holder

2 Timothy 1:7 "For God has not given us a spirit of fear, but one of power, love, and sound judgment."

I attended a conference during the Season of Covid. As I write this, I do not know how long this season will last, nor do I know at what point you will be reading this, but at the time of the conference, Covid was definitely a thing.

The people in charge of the conference had communicated clearly that masks would be mandatory at all times, except during meals. Okay, people have differing convictions on the subject of masks, but attendance at the conference was not compulsory, and the people in charge had made clear what their policy would be.

When we arrived at the conference, however, the organizers began singing a different tune. We were all sitting at tables in a large room. After encouraging us to keep our masks on because they did not want us to become a super spreader event, the leader went on to say that we should work it out with the people at our tables regarding whether or not we would stay masked. We spent several hours in that room together. It was big, and we were spread out, but we were experiencing a lot of face-to-face hours.

The longer the meetings dragged on, the more people were taking their masks off.

Before getting to the point here, let me be clear about what the point is not: a discussion on the reliability of masks vs. Covid. This devotion is not about whether or not masks work all the time, some of the time, or none of the time.

This is about saying what we are going to do and then doing it. Interestingly, one of the topics at the conference was on the importance of having hard conversations and dealing with conflict. Because the organizers made it clear that they were not going to enforce their own rules, it put some of the conference-goers in an awkward spot. There could have been people in attendance who were concerned about their health—maybe they had risky preexisting conditions, or they were concerned about passing the disease on to a vulnerable loved one. Such attendees had spent their money, and they were committing their time, and they were put in an uncomfortable situation.

Did anyone complain? Did anyone go home early? I don't know, and that is fine because really it was none of my business how other people chose to handle their situation. But from a leadership standpoint, I wish the organizers had stuck to their own clearly stated policies.

But what about us? Do we shy away from important conversations because we just do not want to deal with the blowback? Do we compromise on our principles at work or with loved ones because we do not want to create an awkward situation? Let us pray today for the resolve to speak a hard truth or make a difficult stand whenever necessary.

Day 19

The Word

by Jill Holder

2 Timothy 3:14-16 "But as for you, continue in what you have learned and firmly believed. You know those who taught you, and you know that from infancy you have known the sacred Scriptures, which are able to give you wisdom for salvation through faith in Christ Jesus. All Scripture is inspired by God and profitable for teaching, for rebuking, for training in righteousness."

When my son was a little boy, he became so excited on Easter to find his first little picture Bible in his Easter basket! He would sit and look at it for hours, learning all the Bible stories even before he could read all the words. Over the years, he had many Bibles, including the small one that he carried in his back pocket when he went to a public high school and a brown leather one that currently sits on my bedside table, reminding me of him while he lives thousands of miles away. Some of his Bibles were small, some large, some thin line, some hardback versions with pictures. He even used a couple of paperback copies for Bible classes at school. The common thread is that they were all *God-breathed!*

Some people argue that surely scribes must have changed Scripture over thousands of years, somehow diminishing its validity. However, copies of the Bible dating back to the fourteenth century AD are almost identical to today's Scriptures. When the Dead Sea Scrolls were examined, they were found to be almost identical to our Bible. At most, only one percent of the Scriptures have changed, mostly in wording such as "Jesus Christ" instead of "Christ Jesus." None of the doctrine is jeopardized. Why is this a surprise? Surely a God who can part the Red Sea and raise a man from the dead can protect His Word.

I have heard of prisoners of war who clung to the Scriptures that they memorized, sharing them with other prisoners. I have read of Christians in other countries that risk their lives to have a few hidden pages of the Bible because it is that valuable to them. We are so fortunate that we have always had easy access to the Bible our entire lives! We can read it anytime, day or night. Not only that, but many of us have had the benefit of biblical teaching by family members who loved God and followed Him in difficult times. We have been blessed to have biblical instruction by pastors and Christian leaders readily available to us.

In the hard times, Scripture is a lifeline. But the challenge is to remember how much we need it every day! As Paul advised Timothy in 2 Timothy 1:14, "Guard the good deposit through the Holy Spirit who lives in us." May we do the same today.

Day 20

Cynicism

by Timothy D. Holder

2 Corinthians 5:17 "Therefore, if anyone is in Christ, he is a new creation; the old has passed away, and see, the new has come!"

For those who have only known me since I moved to Tennessee, it might come as a surprise that there are times when I struggle with a spirit of cynicism.

For those who have known me longer, it probably does not surprise them at all.

I am much less cynical these days, but I realized recently that I can still be prone to such sentiments. I am vulnerable to thinking this way when these three factors are in play: when I am tired, exposed to something new, and surrounded by people I do not know. That seems to be the toxic brew that brings out my old baggage.

Does this mean I have been living a lie? Am I still the same old person but pretending to be someone different?

I prefer to believe that what I am is a work in progress. And I am encouraged by two things. I was surprised when my recent feelings of cynicism kicked in, which meant I was no longer used to having them. Also, instead of just wallowing in cynicism, I prayed that God would forgive me and give me a better attitude about the situation that prompted it.

God is still in the process of sanctifying me, as I continue along the process of becoming a new creation. I believe I am a better man today than I was yesterday, and tomorrow I can grow some more. That is my prayer for today, and I hope it is yours too.

Day 21

Grit

by Timothy D. Holder

Luke 21:19 "By your endurance, gain your lives."

    I made a big mistake one day during Covid Season. Masks in grocery stores had been a thing for a good two months on the day of my incident. It started with me just needing five items. I wasn't even going to get a basket, much less a buggy, because I figured I could just hold everything in my hands. I had already picked up three of my items, and I was in the back of the store when I realized my mistake: I forgot to wear a mask.
    Who forgets to wear a mask in a grocery store after doing it for two months? Apparently, this guy does.
    What was I supposed to do? I could have set down my three items and walked all the way through the store to go out to my car and get my mask. But that would make me look like a jerk for setting down stuff where it didn't belong. The only way I could leave it all with an employee would be if I chose to talk to a stranger in public while not wearing a mask, so I did not want to do that.
    What could I do?
    As swiftly as possible, I got my remaining items, headed for the self-checkout, and avoided eye contact with everyone along the way.
    There are times in life when the only way out is through. We mess up, sometimes by honest mistakes and sometimes as a result of bad judgment, but we cannot always choose to just shut down, quit, or walk away. There are times in life, and more relevantly to us here when working for the Lord, when we just need to gut it out and

get it done. Let us pray today for the grit to push through our mistakes and missteps and complete the task before us.

Day 22

Choices

by Timothy D. Holder

Proverbs 12:15 "A fool's way is right in his own eyes, but whoever listens to counsel is wise."

A while back, I had a bird that kept flying into my glass sliding door over and over again. I could not decide who was being tortured worse—the bird who was hurting itself or me having to hear the recurring and nonrhythmic thudding sound as it smacked against the glass.

I wrote about my situation on social media, and someone suggested I put something on the glass so the bird would see that it was not an area he could fly through. I taped my census notice up, and it did not immediately solve the issue one hundred percent, but eventually the problem went away.

After a few months, I took the paper down, and everything was fine for a while. This morning in a span of less than two minutes, a bird flew into the glass sliding door four times.

The lesson for the day is obvious: Birds are stupid.

I guess there is a reason that "bird brain" is an insult, but we never call a person a "cat brain" or a "chimpanzee brain."

What is interesting, though, is we are often like my backyard bird. We engage in the same behavior, over and over, despite the fact that it hurts us. Maybe it is an addiction problem, perhaps it is an attraction to the same type of dysfunctional personality, or it could be an indulgence in a character trait that drives people away (like anger or selfishness or complaining).

Let us pray today for the wisdom to make smart choices and turn away from the lure of familiar but hurtful behaviors.

Day 23

Bravery

by Jill Holder

2 Chronicles 20:15-17 "And he said, 'Listen carefully, all Judah and you inhabitants of Jerusalem and King Jehoshaphat. This is what the Lord says: "Do not be afraid or discouraged because of this vast number, for the battle is not yours, but God's. Tomorrow, go down against them. You will see them coming up the Ascent of Ziz, and you will find them at the end of the valley facing the Wilderness of Jeruel. You do not have to fight this battle. Position yourselves, stand still, and see the salvation of the Lord. He is with you, Judah and Jerusalem. Do not be afraid or discouraged. Tomorrow, go out to face them, for the Lord is with you."

These verses in 2 Chronicles have become very dear to me over the years. They are highlighted, starred, and marked with a Post-it Tab in my Bible. Why? Over and over, I have dealt with fear. It's been one of my greatest weaknesses. But the knowledge that I do not have to fight the battle, but rather stand firm as God fights on my behalf, has made *all* the difference.

Years ago, I heard of the testimony of John Paton and his wife, who were missionaries to the Hebrides Islands. Christianity was viewed with hostility by the natives, and one night the Patons found their mission headquarters surrounded by a tribe that threatened to burn down their house and kill them. They prayed all night, and when the sun came up in the morning, the natives were no longer there.

A year later the chief of the tribe accepted Christ. Mr. Paton eventually asked him why the tribe had not followed through with the violence they had planned against him and his wife that night. The chief revealed that the natives had left because they were afraid of the hundreds of big men with drawn swords standing guard around the mission. While Mr. and Mrs. Paton prayed that night, God was fighting the battle on their behalf.

My father mentioned recently that he mowed a field where sheep graze. When the tractor enters the field, the sheep frantically run away in fear. However, they have a close relationship with their owner, and when she is present, they stay close to her and remain calm. Sheep are fearful creatures, easily startled. However, as they encounter fearful situations, they learn to run to the shepherd and stand with her, secure in the knowledge that she will fight on their behalf. They don't have to devise a plan to protect themselves; they just need to stand firm with the shepherd who will protect them.

It is easy to see why we are compared to sheep so many times in Scripture. We have many of the same tendencies to be afraid. But even in the darkest valleys God can be our source of strength; we can find courage and peace in Him. Letting go of trying to protect myself is difficult until I realize that my capabilities are inadequate compared to allowing God to protect me. Only then can I rest in Him and watch the miracles unfold.

In John 16:33, Jesus says, "I have told you these things so that in Me you may have peace. You will have suffering in this world. Be courageous! I have conquered the world."

Let us pray today that we would find our confidence in Christ.

Day 24

Communication

by Timothy D. Holder

1 Corinthians 14:9 "In the same way, unless you use your tongue for intelligible speech, how will what is spoken be known?"

A newscaster put himself in an awkward spot. I was watching a bloopers video online, and it showed a series of mishaps on news programs. In the one I am referencing, the guy at the desk introduced a segment, and then the screen split to show him and a female colleague who was reporting in remotely.

They bantered back and forth, and then the conversation took an unexpected turn. It went something like this:

Him: Okay, we need to stop canoodling now.

Her: What?

Him: I said we need to stop canoodling. (He touched the piece in his ear) What? Oh!

Her: I'm not going to canoodle with you. I have never canoodled with you.

Him: Well...It's a good thing I have a producer in my ear. I would have carried the idea through the entire segment.

Her: What did you think "canoodle" meant?

Him: I thought it meant, like, chatting.

For the record, "to canoodle" means "to cuddle and kiss." The newscaster was guilty of using words he did not know the meaning of.

Do we do this in church sometimes? Do we pray with language we do not quite understand, but we do it because it sounds churchy? Or, on a related note, do we try to share our faith with nonbelievers by using words they are not familiar with?

Words have specific meanings. Let us be good stewards of our words today. May we use words in our prayers that make sense to us, and may we use words with nonbelievers that make sense to them.

Day 25

Holiness

by Timothy D. Holder

1 Peter 1:15 "But as the One who called you is holy, you also are to be holy in all your conduct."

When I was a high school student, many years ago, I had a teacher who was, well, not my favorite. One day, we were all working on an assignment, and she had said since we were doing self-directed work, we could quietly come up to her desk, she would read our palms, and then we could go back to work.

Palm reading. Seriously. I found that to be rather off-putting, but my friend persuaded me to let her read mine. When I had expressed my skepticism to him, saying she would not know anything about us from looking at our palms, he suggested that I prove her wrong then.

Challenge accepted!

When she read my palm, she said—among other things—that I was not very religious.

Me: Well, I got you there.
Her: What do you mean?
Me: I'm a Christian.
Her: Maybe you're a hypocrite.

I was speechless. I had no comeback. In my defense, I was fourteen.

To her point: If I was a Christian, why did I let her read my palm?

Let us pray today for the resolve to not engage in foolish and unchristian things. Let us pray for the resolve to not allow ourselves to be talked into behaviors we know we are not supposed to engage in.

Day 26

Faith

by Jill Holder

Hebrews 11:1 "Now faith is the reality of what is hoped for, the proof of what is not seen."

I sat by the pool and watched my five-year-old son play with his friend. While his buddy confidently swam and splashed in the deep end of the pool, my son stood on the edge, unsure of the water and unable to swim. The boy in the water repeatedly tossed a ball to him, and my son caught it and threw it back. Each time he stepped forward to throw the ball, his feet inched closer and closer to the edge. I warned him to be careful or he would fall into the deep water.

Just as I told his friend's mom that my son was going to fall in any second, he stepped too close to the edge and in he went! Of course, I dove straight into the pool and brought him to the surface, reassuring him calmly that he was safe. Fully dressed and mascara running down my face, I stayed with him in the water for a while to get through the fear that I was sure my boy would need to overcome. But I was wrong. I asked him what happened, and he answered, "I went under the water. I opened my eyes, saw bubbles, and thought, *My mom will save me.*"

I was totally blown away by the faith that my son had in me. I still am! I thought deeply about it for a long time afterward. If my son could have such faith in me, an imperfect and fallible mom, then how much more faith should I have in a perfect God?

It's easy to have faith when our circumstances are good and life is easy. It's when trouble comes that our faith is tested. Job's faith was certainly tested as he lost his children, possessions, and health all in one season. Yet he was able to say, "I know You can do anything, and no plan of Yours can be thwarted...I had heard reports about You, but now my eyes have seen You." (Job 42:2, 5). God is in the business of delivering His people, just as He delivered the Israelites from Pharaoh's army by parting the Red Sea.

I have found that the moment when the waters of trouble swirl around me is when I most need to cling to faith. And each time God delivers me from the struggle, my faith grows. One of my favorite quotations is by Charles Spurgeon, who wrote, "The Lord will make a way for you where no foot has been before. That which threatens to drown you will be a highway for your escape."

Let us pray today for faith that God will see us through the trials we will face.

Day 27

Encouragement

by Timothy D. Holder

1 Chronicles 28:20 "Then David said to his son Solomon, 'Be strong and courageous, and do the work. Don't be afraid or discouraged for the Lord God, my God, is with you. He won't leave you or abandon you until all the work for the service of the Lord's house is finished.'"

Most of us can benefit from a healthy dose of encouragement every now and again. I certainly could have when I worked as a bellringer for the Salvation Army during my days as a college student.
Students at my school, Asbury, were recruited to work for various Salvation Army Corps from all over America through the Christmas season. This was because, unlike many colleges, we had a school break from before Thanksgiving until after New Years' Day. Thus, we could stand outside of grocery stores and department stores for weeks on end, ringing a bell or playing an instrument, and invite people to donate money for the needy.
One of the things I enjoyed about the work was that it was an opportunity to go off to some city I had never been to and experience life with a bunch of college friends. But the job itself could be a grind. A regular shift might be 10 AM to 8 PM, and since they would go through the city dropping off a full van of students one by one, some of us were on-site much longer than that. Other than meal and bathroom breaks, we just stood out there in the cold, trying to smile and make eye contact with strangers as we rang bells or played instruments. FYI, I played some harmonica.
We put in these long hours six days a week for several weeks. And for the young version of me—whose

glass was half-empty and who was sorely lacking in grit—getting out of the van, leaving my friends, and stepping into the cold each day was a discouraging event.

On one such morning, I exited the vehicle, turned around to face my friends, and said, "Think happy thoughts." Then, I slammed the door shut and moved into my position in front of a Kmart or wherever I was that day.

One of the young ladies on the van thought that was quite the dose of encouragement. She began saying it to everyone as they got off the van. She ended the practice within a few days, probably because I rained on her parade by telling her I was being sarcastic when I originally said it.

In retrospect, I wish I had just let her offer the encouragement. We have enough negativity and sarcasm in the world. And what is the value of such things in the lives of Christians? I have seen people come to Christ by various means, but I have never seen someone get "sarcasmed" into the Kingdom of God.

Are we positive influences in our environment? Do we build people and things up, or do we tear them down?

Let us pray today to be salt and light in a world that is desperate for both. Let's be encouragers.

Day 28

More

by Timothy D. Holder

2 Corinthians 9:8 "And God is able to make every grace overflow to you so that in every way, always having everything you need, you may excel in every good work."

There have been a few occasions in my life when I have been asked some variation of the question, "When do you feel closest to God?" My answer: when I preach.

Perhaps weirdly, while I can sometimes be a little reticent to talk much around strangers, I am wired for mass communication. I am comfortable with getting up and speaking in front of big groups, and it does not matter to me if I know the people or not.

It is a lot of work to get in front of people and preach, give a speech, or teach a class. I have to write the message, of course, but I will also fully practice it out loud several times. If it is a sermon, and sometimes even if it is not, I also pray about it.

Why do I put so much time into sermons specifically? It's like I said above: God made me for this kind of thing, and doing it makes me feel closest to Him.

Interestingly, I have been blessed in a way I did not anticipate. I have preached at Cold Spring Church in Bristol a handful of times each year for the last several years. I preached nine times at Snow Memorial Baptist Church in Johnson City during fall 2019, and I was the interim pastor at Alder Branch Baptist in Sevierville more recently. The thing about all three of these experiences is I have received much more than I anticipated. I expected that I would go into each place and feel blessed by the opportunity to preach, and I was. But I was also blessed by the love of the people. I figured with my limited involvement, I would not really get to know them, and they would not get to know me, but in each church, I was touched by the warmth and love of the people.

This is one of the things that happens when we are faithful to our calling. God blesses us in ways we do not foresee. For years I have heard people say, "You can't out give God," and this is how I have seen that truism manifested in my life.

Let us today thank God for blessing us in ways we do not anticipate, especially when we busy ourselves with serving Him.

PS: By the way, I did not mention the blessing that my longtime home church of Wallace has been to me, simply because it did not fit the profile of what I was talking about. I was quite involved at Wallace for many years, I got to know the people well, and there was nothing surprising about the love that church showed me. It was overwhelming at times (always in a good way), but it was never surprising.

Day 29

Direction

by Jill Holder

Proverbs 3:5-6 "Trust in the Lord with all your heart, and do not lean on your own understanding; in all your ways know Him, and He will make your paths straight."

As a competitive cheerleader, my daughter had experienced a wonderful weekend at her out-of-town competition. Her cheer team's hard work had paid off, and they received a six-foot-tall trophy and grand champion banner to prove it. Elated, she and I were ready to head back home to Knoxville. We filled the tank with gasoline, grabbed supper at a fast-food restaurant, and climbed back into the car, chatting excitedly about the team victory and about life in general.

I turned onto the dark interstate that Sunday night and remember remarking about how nice it was that this competition was so close to home, just a ninety-minute drive, unlike other competitions that were hours away. Plus, I had driven the route from Chattanooga dozens of times over the years, so I knew the way and could relax and have a great time with my daughter as we drove.

About thirty minutes later, I vaguely noticed a road sign indicating the distance to Atlanta, which I thought was strange since Atlanta was in the opposite direction, but we were listening to music and laughing, so I ignored the thought and drove on. An hour into the trip, another road sign read "Atlanta 48 miles". Wait. What?

It slowly dawned on us that I had been driving in the wrong direction for the last hour. The energy in our car quickly deflated as we realized that we were not almost home. Instead, we were two and a half hours away. My blunder would cause us to get home extremely late that night with a very early morning for both of us the next day. We were both exhausted and barely awake as we finally pulled into our driveway.

So, what happened? I had failed to consult the directions when I chose the path home. I thought I knew where I was going. I had even gone this way before, so I didn't even look at the road signs and wrongly chose the route that took us even farther away from our destination. Now, the kids routinely ask me on road trips if I am going in the right direction and I have learned the importance of seeking guidance for the journey.

Similarly, in choosing a path for our lives, we must remember that God has the perfect roadmap for the way we should go. His directions are far better than our own understanding, even if we have traveled a certain way before. Just as I should have paused to seek direction from the road signs or my GPS, we need to pause and seek direction from Him in our life. Let us pray today and do just that.

Day 30

Discipleship

by Timothy D. Holder

Luke 9:23 "Then He said to them all, 'If anyone wants to follow after Me, let him deny himself, take up his cross daily, and follow Me.'"

I like to work out. I am not a gym rat with an age-defying physique, but I work out regularly, which keeps me in better shape than I would otherwise be.

Okay, maybe it was an overstatement to say that I *like* to work out. It is actually kind of boring to me. But if I put in a DVD of something I enjoy watching, then I can work out and not feel like I am wasting time.

I am also pretty careful about what I eat. My blood sugar was getting a little high, so my doctor sent me to a nutritionist. She started explaining to me how certain foods convert into, um, sugar or whatever and impact our blood. I said, "Okay, honestly? I've got a friend, Jonathan Hodge, who is a professional counselor, and he told me I was the most goal-oriented person he has ever known. You don't need to explain things to me. Just tell me what I can eat, and I will eat it."

Here's the thing: I could have a really good workout one time, and that would be nice, but it would not lead to any kind of long-term improvement in my health. And I could be super careful about what I eat for a couple of days, but that would not permanently lower my blood sugar.

And so it is with our Christian walk. One mountaintop experience does not make us invulnerable to temptation and sin. We have to choose to follow Christ and engage in our spiritual disciplines daily. Let us pray today for the fortitude to continue on the path of discipleship.

Day 31

Selfishness

by Timothy D. Holder

Philippians 2:4 "Everyone should look not to his own interests, but rather to the interests of others."

One Sunday afternoon when I was a kid, my dad and I were at a golf course. He was there to hit a bucket of balls, and I was on the practice green. He loved to play golf, but I just liked to putt. We were only going to be there for a little while, though, because later that day the British Open was going to be on TV. Since it was, of course, played in Great Britain, it was on tape delay.

I was excited that year: My favorite golfer, Jack Nicklaus, was tied for the lead going into the last round.

The green I was putting on was huge. It had several golf holes on it so several people could practice putting at once. And on that day, it was pretty crowded. I remember, even though it was more than forty years ago, one guy asked another if he was going to watch the Open.

The other man replied, "No, I heard on the radio that Watson won, so why bother watching the replay?"

At the time, all I felt was disappointment that my guy came in second. But looking back on it, I am struck by the selfishness of the second man. I am sure his intent was not to ruin the viewing experience of everyone within earshot, but he did. He complained that he had no more incentive to watch the broadcast, but by being so indiscrete, he robbed us of our incentive as well.

I cannot help but wonder how often we do something similar. It is not that we are trying to hurt someone else, but how often are we so focused on our own

Devotions for a New Day

business that we are oblivious to what our choices are doing to someone else?

Let us pray today that the Lord would make us sensitive to what our words and deeds are doing to those around us.

Day 32

Pride

by Timothy D. Holder

Proverbs 16:18 "Pride comes before destruction, and an arrogant spirit before a fall."

As I was watching the Super Bowl in 2021, the Tampa Bay Buccaneers began to pull away from the Kansas City Chiefs, and the score got lopsided. At some point in the second half, as the Bucs were thoroughly in command, I saw a Bucs defender stand over a downed Chief and make a gesture that the refs labeled as "taunting." A flag was thrown, and a penalty was assessed.

I thought it was a classless move by the Buccaneer defender. Pride is an ugly thing.

I later learned that the gesture he used was one the Chiefs player made whenever he scored a touchdown. I am sure that made it sting all the more. If the Chiefs player had not been rubbing it in all season, he might not have been on the receiving end of it in the Super Bowl.

We could get into the weeds on the subject of football players celebrating vs. taunting and where that line should be drawn, but that is, of course, not the point.

The point is, as I wrote above, that pride is an ugly thing. If we display it, how in the world will people be receptive if we then turn around and try to communicate Christ? Jesus was a servant, and He is our role model. Let us today examine our hearts for pride, and may we repent as needed.

Day 33

Instructions

by Jill Holder

Proverbs 8:33 "Listen to instruction and be wise; don't ignore it."

It was a beautiful day at Disney World, and Tim and I were having a wonderful time together. We had plans to enjoy the parks with another couple (Tim's oldest brother, Jim, and his wife, Sandy), but since we had arrived ahead of them, we had gone on into the Magic Kingdom to experience as many rides as possible before the anticipated larger crowds came later in the day. That morning, we went straight to our personal favorites, Small World and The Hall of Presidents, and then enjoyed Peter Pan's Flight with almost no wait time. Fun!

After enjoying more of the park, we decided that it was time for lunch and headed to The Columbia Harbour House, which is located next to Peter Pan's Flight. We paused at the door and acknowledged the posted sign informing us that the restaurant was closed. However, we also saw that there was a line inside and agreed that we had really wanted to eat there and had even *planned* to eat there. We both love a good plan, so we went inside anyway and got in line.

For the next twenty minutes, we had a great time standing in line together, talking and laughing as we threaded through the restaurant, before we realized that all the seating areas were closed. When we got closer to the food counters, we saw that those were closed as well. We confirmed our suspicions with a helpful Disney employee who told us that, yes, the sign outside was correct. The restaurant was closed, and we had been standing in the overflow line for Peter Pan's Flight, which we had already ridden that morning. As we slipped out through a side door, we both agreed that we should not have ignored the notice on the sign.

Many of us would say that we are good at seeking instruction for our lives. We listen to the pastor give us instruction at church and we may even take notes. We hear biblical teaching on the car radio. There is wisdom in the faith-based music on our playlists. We even read Scripture in the search for direction from God for our lives, but do we heed the guidance that we have been given, or are we choosing to ignore it in favor of doing what we want to do anyway?

In the case of Tim and I ignoring the sign that directed us that the restaurant was closed, we were able to laugh because there were no devastating consequences. But dismissing the directions and guidance that we receive from God has far worse implications than ignoring a sign from Disney World. Instructions from the Lord prevent us from falling into the deep pitfalls that can be severely damaging to us and often to those who love us as well.

So, let us pray today to not be just hearers of God's Word and instructions, but also people who take them to heart and follow them.

Day 34

Holiness

by Timothy D. Holder

1 Peter 1:16 "For it is written, 'Be holy as I am holy.'"

Jill wrote in the last devotion about our trip to Disney World. There are four things I would like to make clear about the experience. One, It's a Small World is her favorite ride. Two, The Hall of Presidents is mine. Three, though we do like the slower stuff, we enjoy the roller coasters too.

Four, and most importantly, because we were not yet married, we stayed in separate rooms. I would not have asked her otherwise, and she would not have joined me on the trip if I had not said we would be in separate rooms.

I write this not in an effort to sound holier than thou, but I do want to model holiness. God loves us, but that does not mean He wants us to do whatever we want. We are called to be holy—to be blameless and set apart.

The world might tell us we deserve to be happy and we should do whatever is required to make it so. But the Bible has a different message. The world might tell us what we do is no one's business but our own. The Bible does not say that either.

The Bible tells us to be holy, and if that contradicts what I think will make me happy, so be it. The Bible tells us that if we follow Christ, we are part of a body of believers, so what I do is the business of other people—my actions impact them.

Let us pray today that God will help us strive for holiness.

Day 35

Companionship

by Timothy D. Holder

Ecclesiastes 4:12 "And if someone overpowers one person, two can resist him. A cord of three strands is not easily broken."

There is one more thing I would like to share about my trip to Disney World with Jill. I had no intention of compromising on my policy of separate rooms, but it certainly made things easier that Jill was one hundred percent in agreement with me. It might have become a temptation to lower my standards if her convictions had been different.

It would have been easy to rationalize sharing a room. "It would save money to just share a room, and God wants us to be good stewards of our money." "We know we won't cross the line, and if we did, separate rooms wouldn't stop us anyway, so what difference does it make?" "No one back home will know if we're in one room or two."

But purity in this area is important, and it is a way to honor God. It is certainly easier to maintain one's convictions when those convictions are shared by the other person.

We need to not isolate ourselves from the world. How could we communicate the Gospel to people if we are isolated from them? But when it comes to our most important relationships, we need some believers in the mix. We are all fallible, so we need people who will keep us accountable.

Let us pray today for ever-stronger relationships with other Christians.

Day 36

Discernment

by Jill Holder

Acts 17:11 "The people here were of more noble character than those in Thessalonica, since they received the Word with eagerness and examined the Scriptures daily to see if these things were so."

If you swallow a watermelon seed, one will grow in your stomach.
Knocking on wood three times will make a positive statement come true.
Walking on top of the graves in the cemetery brings bad luck.
If you tell someone about your nightmare before breakfast, it will come true.
Find a penny, pick it up, and all day long, you'll have good luck.
My family's roots run deep in the Appalachian foothills of Tennessee, so superstitious sayings were as much a part of my upbringing as the accent floating in the air around us. We all knew that walking under a ladder brought bad luck, dropping the dishcloth meant that company was coming soon, and all wishes on shooting stars would come true. Personally, I became skilled at jumping over all sidewalk cracks as a little girl under the guise of protecting my mother's back from breaking.
My grandmother, Nora Jackson, was once given a willow tree sapling by her nephew, Maynard. A couple of years later, Maynard went off to war. As the war raged and the tree grew, she recalled the saying that when a willow tree grows tall enough to cast a shadow the size of a grave, the one who planted it will die. Did she believe the saying?

Who knows, but she chopped the tree down just to be safe. Maynard eventually returned from the war and there are still no willow trees on the property to this day.

Sometimes there was wisdom in the sayings; sometimes not so much. A red sky in the morning does often signal a sailor to take warning. Opening an umbrella in the house really is bad luck to the person who gets poked in the eye. And one of my least favorites as a child, waiting to run barefoot through the fresh spring grass until after May 10th when the ground is warmer, does have merit. On the other hand, I seriously doubt that placing a knife underneath the bed of a woman in childbirth will cut the pain. We have to look at what we hear and filter it through our knowledge of truth.

The same is true for what we have been told about God. Many teachers and preachers are readily available to us through the internet, social media, and in our churches. Our friends and family may share their views on the Lord. Sometimes these opinions don't coincide, so how do we know what is true? We must filter what we hear through our knowledge of what Scripture says, and the only way to fully know what the Bible says is to follow the example of the Bereans and read it daily, examining it and learning it so that we may grow in spiritual discernment. May we devote ourselves to the study of God's Word!

Day 37

Communication

by Timothy D. Holder

Proverbs 25:11 "A word spoken at the right time is like apples in silver settings."

Earlier in the book, I told a story about how dramatic my car trip was the first time I was supposed to go to church with Jill. I now present you, dear reader, with another story from that day.

We were sitting next to each other in church that morning. We were wearing masks because it was during the Season of Covid. I wanted to communicate something to her, but because it was our first time sitting in church together, I did not know how she felt about talking during the service. I used my rudimentary sign language skills to get my message across. Despite the mask on her face, I knew she was smiling. I could see it in her eyes.

She leaned in toward me and whispered, "I love you too."

It was sweet, it was wonderful, and it was reciprocated. But I could not help but chuckle as I whispered softly back to her, "I spelled out 'g-u-m.'"

For the record, I also made it clear I loved her, too, but it begs the question of how often we miscommunicate, even with those close to us. Do we sometimes communicate a message of judgment and condemnation to people who instead need the Gospel and hope? Let us pray that the love of Christ would grow in us today and that we would communicate that love clearly to the world around us.

Day 38

Humor

by Timothy D. Holder

Ecclesiastes 3:4A "...a time to weep and a time to laugh..."

Late one afternoon, I sent an email to the dean of the library at Walters State, Jamie Posey. I needed to ask him about a George Washington book. At the bottom of the email, I shifted gears and asked, "Have you seen my cell phone?"

The next morning, I had an hour-long meeting at work. I mention this because during that time I was not monitoring my email. When I got out of the meeting and checked my messages, I was greatly dismayed to see four from the librarians.

Jamie had started the thread by asking his colleagues if they had seen a missing cell phone. Several minutes later, Julie Lewis replied that she would look around on the first floor. Then Audrey Shoemaker said she had to go to the faculty reading room for something, so she would check there. Finally, Chasity Brogan emailed to say that she had been looking for thirty minutes and could not find it, so she was just going to call campus police.

I immediately fired off a reply. "Oh, my goodness! I was making a joke with Jamie because years ago, I thought I lost my phone in the library, but it was in my bag, and sometimes he teases me about it. I'm so sorry for all your trouble."

A few minutes later I followed up with an email that read, "You guys are just messing with me, aren't you?"

They were.

It was fun, and it was funny. And it says something about Jamie and his staff. In many cases, we can choose to enjoy our work and find the humor in our situations. What an impact we can have on the world today if we simply choose to display a good mood. We don't have to be slaves to our feelings; we can choose to be pleasant. Let us pray today that we would be a light in the world simply by choosing to be good company.

Day 39

His Presence

by Jill Holder

Isaiah 41:10 "Do not fear, for I am with you; do not be afraid, for I am your God. I will strengthen you; I will help you; I will hold on to you with My righteous hand."

As a mom of three kids, I was elated to be pregnant with a fourth little blessing. I wasn't new to being pregnant, I knew what to expect, and this pregnancy was no different than the previous ones. I had suffered the morning sickness that lasted all day and night. There was discomfort, a sore back, and food had lost its taste, but these were all just necessary facets of bringing a new life into the world and totally worth it.

I went in for a routine ultrasound with the reassurance that my baby had been wiggling the night before. The friendly nurse set up the ultrasound machine and began the very familiar process of squirting the warm gel on my growing belly and searching for my little baby on the monitor. As the image came into view, I noticed right away that something was wrong. There was no heartbeat.

Before I looked into the kind face of the nurse to affirm my fear, before she left to get the doctor, before I lay on the exam table with the growing realization of the loss, and before I could even call out to God, I felt His presence in that room. He was already there.

The next few days were difficult. As I explained to my children that God had healed our baby by taking it to heaven, called close family members with the news, and went back to the hospital for an outpatient procedure, God's presence was very real, giving me strength. I moved as if in a fog, my arms feeling empty as I longed to hold my baby, but at the same time there was a constant deep feeling of peace from the Lord that never left.

As I look back on those times, it is clear that my experience is just one of many examples throughout time that God's promise in Isaiah is true. He is always with us, holding us and strengthening us. He is always present even *before* we know that we need Him. He is there even *before* we call on His name. Let us pray today that we are aware of His faithful presence in our lives.

Day 40

Pride

by Timothy D. Holder

Isaiah 2:12 "For a day belonging to the Lord of Armies is coming against all that is proud and lofty, against all that is lifted up—it will be humbled."

Major League Baseball is different from other professional sports. People have said that and written it on multiple occasions. From Spring Training through the World Series, the season lasts more than half a year, and teams average about six games a week. As a result, the mental grind is different from other major sports. This is why some people say baseball managers have to spend more time managing egos. If a ballplayer gets too beaten down by the workload and the pressure, then his discouragement might spread through the clubhouse.

This became even more interesting to me when I further learned that baseball managers will favor aging veterans over younger players who might be more productive. The argument went that the veteran was more important to the clubhouse psyche, so the vet needed to keep starting, even though he was not as productive.

What really *really* made this interesting to me recently was reading that other professions are like this. A writer described a situation where a young teacher won her school's Teacher of the Month Award, and it hurt morale because the veteran teachers were unhappy. The inference the writer made was that a smart administrator would have chosen a veteran teacher because that teacher would have more influence over morale in the building.

I thought that was appalling. If I do not win an award that is important to me, then I need to do my job better, not get jealous of a younger person who earned the prize. I mean, what a lack of character. And I write this as someone who has spent thirty years teaching.

What is our attitude in the workplace? Are we self-entitled veterans who feel we deserve preferential treatment? Pride is a pretty unattractive quality. For the Christian, pride is diametrically opposed to the attitude that we are supposed to display. If we struggle with pride or self-entitlement, let us pray today a prayer of repentance for this sin.

Day 41

Imitations

by Timothy D. Holder

Psalm 16:11 "You reveal the path of life to me; in Your presence is abundant joy; at Your right hand are eternal pleasures."

Tom Holland, who plays Spider-Man, tells an interesting story about what it was like to meet Robert Downey Jr, aka Ironman. According to Holland, he was excited to get to talk to the guy who basically launched the Marvel Cinematic Universe. Holland told him what a thrill it was to talk to him, and the younger actor spoke admiringly about Downey's work.

Holland recalled that Downey did not look exactly like Holland expected him to, but Holland just shrugged that off and kept talking to him. Then a door opened and in walked...Robert Downey Jr.

Holland had been talking to RDJ's stunt double!

How often do we settle for an imitation instead of the real thing? As Christians, we say we believe that true happiness can only come from God, but many Christians will then turn around and try to find satisfaction in some other way. Some of us are addicted to the praise or approval of other people. Some struggle with obsessions with food or porn. Drugs, legal and otherwise, have a deadly grip on many.

Let us dedicate ourselves today to focusing on our relationship with Christ. Let us turn away from the sins and distractions that entangle us and find our satisfaction in Him. Let us pray today that we would find our satisfaction in Christ and not in cheap imitations.

Day 42

Action

by Timothy D. Holder

1 Peter 1:13 "Therefore, with your minds ready for action, be sober-minded and set your hope completely on the grace to be brought to you at the revelation of Jesus Christ."

One of the best chess players I have ever gone up against is Garrett Brown. Now, to give you some context, dear reader, I am a pretty fair chess player. I made the team during my last two years in elementary school. Full disclosure: During my first year, I lost every game I played when the team went to the district meet. But in my second year, I was the first seed on our team, which was cool (to me). I think I won a few games that year, but my most vivid memory was my friend sharing some of his grape soda with me in between games. It tasted good.

I digress.

My point is I am a decent chess player. Over the course of my life, I have won more games than I have lost. But then I faced Garrett. I had not played much over the years, but when I was around the age of thirty-nine, our families were on vacation together at the beach, and we had some time on our hands.

What is funny to me is that neither Garrett nor I remember who won the game, but I remember how I felt while I was playing him. I was legitimately a little nervous—something I never felt while playing chess, except maybe during the tournaments.

Garrett provoked such a reaction because he played extremely aggressively. Most of the people I have played outside of the tournaments either wasted moves as they waited to see what would unfold, or they played very defensively. In such cases, they were not trying to win; they were simply playing not to lose. Of course, this greatly diminished their chances for success.

Garrett, on the other hand, was relentless, and he kept me off balance. Admittedly, part of the pressure I felt was not just that he was giving himself a serious shot at winning, but also that, um, well, he was nine years old.

I really did not want to lose to a little kid.

Garrett gave himself a chance to win because he was aggressive, which was a strategy I always employed when playing chess.

But this is not a book about chess. How are we carrying out our responsibilities as Christians? Are we aggressively pursuing the Lord's agenda and striving to succeed at the task at hand, or are we meandering around spiritually, content with just staying in the game and avoiding colossal mistakes? Let us pray today that we would be people of action for the Kingdom of God. Let us be persistent. Let us make the enemy nervous.

Day 43

Heroes

by Jill Holder

Galatians 6:9 "Let us not become weary in doing good, for we will reap at the proper time if we don't give up."

Heroes are not just found on a movie screen.

I met Krystal, Kayelin, Krista, and Samantha on the first day of class at a local ministry, A Hand Up For Women. Each of these ladies and their classmates was working on rebuilding their lives after drug use and jail time had derailed their plans. Our class was focused on learning to become the women that God had always called us to be, and as I began teaching that first evening, I was struck by their expressions. Apprehension was written all over their quiet faces; their struggles had been real, and it showed.

We began dealing with fear, shame, and finding our identity in Christ, and the ladies in the class began to slowly open up. Tears were shed, changes began, and we saw new realizations begin to impact lives. Then COVID hit.

After a two-week break to regroup and form a new plan, we gave virtual classes a try. Accountability is difficult without being together in person, and one by one ladies began dropping out. By the time classes were able to meet again, albeit with attendees wearing masks and socially distancing, the number of students had greatly dwindled. But these four ladies remained, and they kept on coming!

Their path was certainly not an easy one. One lady's cousin passed away in prison, followed by the death of her mother, but she kept coming. Still another gave birth to a baby boy, but she bundled him up and kept coming. Jobs were lost, relationships ended, difficult times came and went, yet they just kept coming two nights a week, every week for an entire year. They also completed homework, met with mentors, learned life skills, and created new friendships and environments for themselves and their children. Most importantly, decisions were made to accept Christ as their Lord and Savior. Many teachers and mentors poured into these women, and they stayed committed to change.

On the day of their graduation from the program, I walked into the room where they were gathered before the ceremony to congratulate these precious ladies and was overwhelmed to the point of tears by what I saw and heard from each of them. Their original expressions of apprehension and silence at the beginning of the program had been replaced with beaming smiles and laughter. I now saw confidence and joy! These ladies had stayed the course, persevered, and were reaping the rewards by stepping into a new future.

Let us pray that we would follow their example of persevering through difficult times. Let us pray that we would follow God, especially when it is not easy.

Day 44

Integrity

by Timothy D. Holder

Proverbs 28:6 "Better the poor person who lives with integrity than the rich one who distorts right and wrong."

Many years ago, when I was young and fairly innocent to the ways of the world, I was a student teacher. It was my first real experience with creating work for students and then grading it.

At one point, I had to explain to a young scholar that I needed to give him a zero. Perturbed by my decision, the student demanded to know why.

I pointed out that he had written the word "iron" for one of his answers.

"So?" His reply was elegant in its simplicity.

"Um," I began, "the right answer was '1904.' But the kid sitting across from you wrote it in such a way that I can see how someone might think he wrote 'iron,' if the person copying it hadn't paid attention to the question."

The perpetrator acknowledged that I caught him, and he took his zero like a champ.

I knew another student a few years ago who told a colleague that he (the student) preferred online classes to traditional ones. He didn't think he would like online classes at first, he said, but then he realized it was easier to cheat in them. The student is a Christian.

We need to be people of integrity. If we give people reason to see us as untrustworthy, then what will happen when we talk about Christ?

Let us pray today that we would be people of integrity, even when we are tempted by ethical shortcuts.

Day 45

Perceptions

by Timothy D. Holder

Hebrews 3:1 "Therefore, holy brothers and sisters, who share in a heavenly calling, consider Jesus, the apostle and high priest of our confession."

When Jimmy Carter was president,[2] he decided to go fishing and relax a little bit. A photographer who had been assigned to him stood from afar, but Carter sat by himself on a canoe in the water.

A nearby rabbit got chased off the shore by some dogs, and it started swimming toward Carter's canoe. The rabbit acted a little strange—maybe it was feral—so Carter used a paddle to force the animal away.

For some reason, one of Carter's aides felt the president's actions demonstrated bravery, and the aide shared the story with a man in the media. Months later, on a slow news day, the story made the front page of a newspaper, accompanied by a picture taken by the photographer.

The presidential aide was mortified when his boss became the subject of ridicule and mockery for using an oar to defend himself against a soft, fluffy bunny rabbit.

Carter had just been minding his own business, and he had not wanted a possibly crazed wild animal on his canoe. The whole thing was really a non-story. Was he brave? Not particularly. Did he deserve contempt for his

---

[2] If you like devotions about presidents, you might be interested in the books *Presidential Stories* or *Devotions with Presidents*.

actions? Not at all. But lots of people had comments that were not flattering.

When we do things—lead, make decisions, accomplish something, etc.—people are going to make judgments. Some might be kind, and the others might be less than that. We cannot control such things.

We should guard against paying too close attention to the opinions of people who do not really know our *what* or our *why*. It can be tempting to hear those voices and react to them, but we would do well to be more concerned about the perception of the One who knows us best and loves us most.

Let us pray today that we can tune out the noise of strangers and acquaintances who do not really know us but judge us anyway. Let us pray today that we will focus solely on pleasing our King.

Day 46

Devotion for a New Day

by Jill Holder

Psalm 118:24 "This is the day the Lord has made; let's rejoice and be glad in it."

A few years ago, to the great disdain of my children, I decided to dive into a deep clean-out and reorganization of all the downstairs closets. I pulled things out for days, repainted walls and shelves, and tossed out more items than any family should own. These were days of chaos, where the kids walked around piles of belongings and retreated to their upstairs bedrooms in the hopes that they would not be roped into the reorganizing madness. When I was finally finished, I sat back and realized two things. One, I really do find fulfillment in organization. Two, I had somehow become a hoarder of candles.

I had a stash of candles of every shape, from tealights and tapers to star shapes and three-wick jars. Tall, short, and in between, I had it covered. There were also candles of many scents, of every season, and for every holiday and special occasion on the Hallmark calendar. I mean, did I really need that many Halloween candles, sparkly red heart candles, and July 4th candles with red, white, and blue stars? I even found floating candles, battery-operated candles, a cat candle, and the list goes on.

It reminded me of a chest of drawers at my grandmother's house. After she passed away, when relatives were cleaning out her home, they found that the chest of drawers in her bedroom was filled with brand new towels, washcloths, and hand towels. Ironic, because the towels that she always used were threadbare and worn while the new ones were sitting in the drawers just a few feet away year after year. While my grandmother had lived through the depression, which probably had affected her saving habits, I had not. I realized that I was just saving the candles for a special day. So, I decided right then that I was no longer waiting for a special day. Today is a special day that the Lord has made! Every day is a day to celebrate!

Now, I burn candles often. It's not unusual to have them lit in multiple rooms all around the house. If I receive a new candle, it goes right to a special table, shelf, or nightstand to be used and enjoyed right away. So, may we pray to always burn the candles, use the best dishes, find the joy, and celebrate the gift of each new day that the Lord has given us!

Day 47

Wise Counsel

by Timothy D. Holder

Proverbs 20:18 "Finalize plans with counsel, and wage war with sound guidance."

There is a guy I know who is great to be around. I always found him to be super easy to talk to. When I was in social situations that would last a long time, I always liked it when this guy was there because a conversation with him was almost effortless.

One day he told me his secret, and I was impressed primarily because I'd had no idea what he had been doing. A typical conversation with him in the fall or early winter might include a discussion about football, and it would go something like this:

Me: Man, Washington just keeps losing. It's *so* frustrating.
Him: I know what you mean. They've been playing *terrible*.
Me: If only their offensive line was better.
Him: Yeah, it's really been holding them back.
Me: It makes me crazy because they have been struggling for years.
Him: I can't remember the last time they were good.

If you think this guy is very agreeable, you are correct, but that is not the full extent of his genius. It was not that he already agreed with me or that he was willing to see it from my point of view; it was that he did not know what I was talking about, so he was just parroting my views back to me. He knew very little about football at all.

But is it any wonder I thought the guy was awesome? I thought I had found my football soul mate.

This friend of mine is happy to agree with me or anybody about things that totally do not matter and where we seem to know more than he does. But I do need to point out that he is a man of integrity, and he does have opinions on subjects with which he is familiar.

What is striking to me is how appealing this trick of his was.

We like people who agree with us, but the reality is this can get us into trouble. Do we ever support people because they say what we want to hear even when it is the opposite of what we need to hear?

Do we care so much about politics that we enjoy it when people on our side insult, ridicule, and lampoon those on the other side? It is satisfying, but is it Christlike? Do we resonate with people who offer us justifications for our sins (lust, greed, gluttony, whatever), even though that contradicts God's Word?

Just because someone's words reinforce our biases and prejudices it does not mean they are good for us. Let us pray today for the insight and fortitude to not be led astray by words that sound great but are not what we need to hear.

Day 48

Mystery

by Timothy D. Holder

1 Corinthians 13:12 "For now we see only a reflection as in a mirror, but then face to face. Now I know in part, but then I will know fully, as I am fully known."

One time I got a gift from my friends Kent and Amy Williams. When I tore off the wrapping, I discovered I was graced with a device that would allow me to watch more TV channels. This was a particularly interesting gift for me because I had gotten rid of cable.

Despite my enthusiasm, I did not take my gift out of its box for several weeks. I had a lot going on, so I did not need something new to watch in the short term, and I am not exactly super tech-savvy. One evening when Jill was visiting, I decided we could try to figure out how to use the equipment together.

It would be a nice teambuilding exercise.

I opened the box, and much to my surprise, it did not contain the device I was expecting.

What I got was a tie.

If you think I suffered a letdown, you are mistaken. I really did not need more TV to watch, and the tie was my favorite color. I loved the personal touch of the gift and the fact that for several weeks I thought I had one thing when I had another. The surprise of it was really cool and funny to me.

There are times in life when we think we are getting one thing, but then we get something else. And so it is with our service to God. We think we have it all figured out and added up—all the plusses and minuses—but then something else unfolds. How often have we said no to an opportunity without saying one prayer about it because we think we know exactly what will happen?

Let us pray today that we will be more open to where God might take us. And while we're at it, let's pray that we won't be such know-it-alls.

Day 49

Effort

by Jill Holder

Colossians 3:23 "Whatever you do, do it from the heart, as something done for the Lord and not for people."

As an actress, I have had the opportunity to meet some wonderful people on set. In my experience, the people in my industry are most often kind, respectful, professional, and truly a pleasure to work with, and I have great respect for many of them. God has brought many sweet friendships into my life through my acting career. However, as in many things, there are exceptions.

In preparation for my role as a detective on a television show, I had spent a significant amount of time with the script memorizing lines, facts, dates, and even the confusing names of medical prescriptions that seemed more like tongue twisters in a foreign language than words that would actually be printed on medicine bottles. When I arrived on set, the actor that I would be interrogating in the upcoming scene was not only late arriving, but he also eventually casually walked in without any apology or explanation for keeping the crew and other actors waiting. After we blocked our scene and received instruction from the director, the slate was clapped, the director called, "Action!", and we began our dialogue. It quickly became apparent that the other actor had absolutely no clue what was going on. As I asked him questions, his answers were bizarre and nonsensical. The director stopped the action, looked at the guy, and asked if he had even read the script.

"Nope," he replied. "I didn't really care about that, so I didn't bother with it."

Things went downhill from there as the rest of us realized this was going to be a slow evening on set. This actor was not prepared. While I have no idea if he was a follower of Christ, it was apparent that he had not given his best effort for the Lord or out of respect for anyone else in this production.

The lesson here is to act the opposite and put forth our best effort. For one thing, in giving our best we will learn and grow to become better versions of ourselves to reach those we meet. Also, wherever we go, we represent the Lord to those around us. In giving our best, we can reflect the example that Christ set in giving His best for us. Let us pray today that we would give our best in all we do, big or small.

Day 50

Secrets

by Timothy D. Holder

1 John 3:3 "And everyone who has this hope in Him purifies himself just as He is pure."

Late one evening, I texted Jill. I had meant to get to sleep early, but I was not able to because I had a lot to do. In my first text, I explained what had kept me up late. Then I followed it with a sweet good-night message that included a declaration of my love for her. And I addressed her with an endearing nickname.

She did not respond, but I just assumed she had already fallen asleep. After midnight, I woke up and looked at my phone. One of Jill's kids was traveling, and he would be arriving at her house late. I saw her message that he was home.

What I did not see were my two messages to her. With a moment of detective work, I discovered, much to my horror, that my messages had gone awry.

I had sent them—the messages that included the testament of my love—to Bradley Thompson.

Now, Bradley is a great guy. He is a young music teacher at a Christian school whom I have had the pleasure of knowing since he was a student at Carson-Newman. I am blessed to call him a friend. But I did not intend for him to receive those messages.

As mentioned above, it was after midnight. A sudden adrenaline spike, courtesy of my careless texting, left me wide awake but not exactly thinking clearly. It was too late at night to send Bradley a clarifying message. Really, though, what had happened would be obvious to him. Nevertheless, my sleep-deprived brain tried to figure out how to "unsend" my message. While I failed in that effort, I did manage to delete years' worth of texts on my own phone, which was…pointless.

The next day, I texted Bradley and apologized for the errant texts. He replied, "Oh, that wasn't for me? Dang, I mean, it's cool if you love me deeply."

While the whole thing was legitimately embarrassing at the time—although I have obviously gotten over it sufficiently enough to write about it here—there was a silver lining: I was not communicating anything to Jill that was immoral, so my witness was not tarnished.

A lot of people get in trouble because of stuff they do on their cell phones. We want to think we can get away with things, but we never know when the truth might be revealed. The way to handle that reality is to strive to be above reproach. The fear of getting caught is not the best reason for living rightly, but it does add a degree of accountability to our thoughts and actions that can be beneficial. Let us pray today that we would feel the incentive to live rightly. Let us send the kind of messages that would not be embarrassing to us if other people read them.

Day 51

Planning

by Timothy D. Holder

Matthew 5:6 "Blessed are those who hunger and thirst for righteousness, for they will be filled."

When I graduated from college, I had a major in Bible and a minor in history. I acquired a lot of knowledge and a few skills in my four years at Asbury. But there was one thing I did not learn, and it really would have been convenient if I had.

I did not know how to cook.

The funny thing is that this really did not occur to me as graduation approached. I had a roommate lined up and a place to live, and those things were important, but I did not think about how I would feed myself.

My parents came to town for my graduation and stayed for a day or so after that, so we went out to eat once or twice and my mother cooked a little. But even at that point my lack of culinary skills was not on my mind. I could have asked my mom some questions, and she would have been very helpful (she's a good mom). It was just not on my radar.

I could scramble eggs, make a salad, and pour a bowl of cereal, but that was about it.

Since these were the days before the internet, looking up recipes online was not an option.

When I eventually realized I had a problem, I solved it by going to the local grocery store, picking out packages of meat, and asking random employees in the meat department how to prepare it.

It still amazes me that I had no plan for something so fundamental.

Are we guilty of this type of approach when it comes to spiritual things? Do we have no plan in place for Bible reading, our prayer life, and/or sharing our faith? These are fundamental things. We need a plan. If we are neglecting any of these things, let us pray today that God would place a plan for improvement on our hearts. I figured out how to cook because I did not want to starve. Let us develop plans for the ancient disciplines of our faith so we do not starve spiritually.

Day 52

Lessons

by Timothy D. Holder

Proverbs 16:16 "Get wisdom—how much better it is than gold! And get understanding—it is preferable to silver."

G. Gordon Liddy worked on the Committee to Reelect the President in 1972. It was called "the CRP" by its supporters and "CREEP" by the opposition. By either name, its one and only function was to help Richard Nixon get reelected. Liddy was one of the many men who went to prison for the Watergate scandal. They ended up there because they were so committed to seeing Nixon's success that they were willing to cross legal lines to ensure that outcome.

Other than Liddy, though, once they got caught, they sang a different tune. They insisted that they were good people who did not mean to do wrong, but they either got caught up in the heat of the moment, or they did some things that they simply did not realize were against the law.

Liddy was different. He knew he was engaging in criminal behavior, and in his autobiography, he acknowledged it. He felt the cause was worth it. There was the Cold War with the Soviets, a hot war in Vietnam, and uncertainty with Cuba and the Middle East. Liddy felt the country needed Nixon, regardless of what Liddy needed to do to keep the man in office.

Liddy was a fascinating person. Part of what made him unique was his willpower. He was quite proud of his strength of will, and he had a peculiar way of demonstrating that will. He would hold his forearm over a flame, either a match or a candle, until his flesh would begin to burn. Why? Just to show how resolute he was.

By the time Liddy went to prison, he had begun feeling a numbness in his arm. When he went to the prison doctor about it, the physician told him it was nerve damage from the repeated burnings. He told Liddy the problem would only get worse unless Liddy quit what he was doing.

Liddy acknowledged the doctor's expertise and the man's instructions. Liddy chose to stop burning his damaged forearm.

The next time he needed to demonstrate the measure of his resolve to someone, Liddy simply burned his other forearm.

It is safe to say that Liddy learned the wrong lesson from his trip to the doctor.

What about us? Sometimes the Lord teaches us lessons through our circumstances. Maybe it is when we feel the consequences of our sins, or it might be when we face adversity. Does the former teach us the value of holiness and the latter help us develop grit? They should.

Unfortunately, sometimes the lesson we take away is that we should be sneakier in our sins. Or we learn that life is not fair to us, and we can get sympathy from some people when we complain a lot and feel sorry for ourselves.

Let us pray today that we would be teachable. Let us humbly ask the Lord for wisdom so something good will be gleaned from difficult life experiences.

Day 53

Sacrifice and Celebration

by Jill Holder

Mark 10:45 "For even the Son of Man did not come to be served, but to serve, and to give His life as a ransom for many."

Sometimes life can begin to resemble organized chaos. Between an acting career, the kids' activities, teaching women, and the various other demands of life, my schedule can go through hectic times where it feels like we have to plan ahead in order to breathe. Especially when multiple days of a full plate are stacked back-to-back, carving out time to spend together as a couple means planning, shifting, and planning again just for a few hours of quality time in the car snatched between call times, band concerts, art exhibits, birthday parties, and the list goes on. You get the picture, possibly because you are in the same boat, which may resemble a sinking ship quickly taking on water.

Thankfully, things are not usually this crazy. But when they are, Tim hangs in there with me. He drives extra trips around town and helps wherever he can. He provides assistance, support, and encouragement. He is patient in the midst of the whirlwind. So, when things settle back down, I enjoy setting aside a special day called "Tim Day". On this day, he gets to choose everything about the day. We go to his favorite restaurants, eat his favorite foods, enjoy the activities he chooses, watch his favorite shows, and generally make the entire day all about him. During an especially hectic month, we sometimes have Tim Day multiple times. Why? Because he has sacrificed so much for the rest of us, and because he is dearly loved, he is honored for the entire day. He smiles and enjoys the fun, and I enjoy helping him know that he is valued and cherished.

Along those lines, when we think of sacrifices made for others, the greatest sacrifice of all was made for us by Jesus when He gave His life for us. Do we set aside time to acknowledge all that He has done for us, or do we take His sacrifice for granted? Are we spending time with Him in prayer and honoring Him with our thoughts and actions? May we pray that every day will be Jesus Day, cherishing Him for who He is and praising Him for the gift of salvation.

*Disclaimer: Lest you think that Tim Days are always only about him, I was surprised with a beautiful engagement ring on a Tim Day, making it a very special day for both of us!

Day 54

Consistency

by Timothy D. Holder

Matthew 6:24 "No one can serve two masters, since either he will hate one and love the other, or he will be devoted to one and despise the other. You cannot serve both God and money."

Several years ago, I read about a man who owned an adult bookstore somewhere in southern Kentucky. He had an encounter with Jesus that changed his life, so he decided that it was wrong for him to be selling his particular set of merchandise.

He took all his products out of the store and burned them. Someone asked him why he did not just sell his inventory to someone else in the industry and take the profits to support himself while he figured out his next career move.

He replied that if he truly felt it was wrong for him to sell that stuff, it would be just as wrong to give someone else the opportunity to sell it. Basically, he decided not to be a hypocrite about it.

Do we approach our choices with the same kind of consistency? Some of us pat ourselves on the back for avoiding Sin A, but refuse to acknowledge that Sin B, which we are wallowing in, is just as bad.

Do we who tithe choose to honor God with our ten percent but then spend part of our ninety percent on vices that would displease Him? We need to be consistent with our money, just as the former adult bookstore owner was consistent in how he handled his resources.

Let us pray today that we would make choices based on integrity when faced with temptations.

Day 55

Temptations

by Timothy D. Holder

1 Corinthians 6:18 "Flee sexual immorality! Every other sin a person commits is outside the body, but the person who is sexually immoral sins against his own body."

As we were driving somewhere in the car one day, Jill told me about someone who had a snake in her house. The woman lost sight of it and moved into a hotel for a couple of days rather than have a sneaky snake slithering around her.

I applaud the woman's problem-solving. I might have considered just selling the house and never coming back.

I might have just burned it to the ground.

Would I really torch my house because there was a snake inside without even knowing if the snake was poisonous? Yes. And I would sleep like a baby.

Okay, maybe that was a little hyperbole. But it is no exaggeration to say the aforementioned woman wanted no part of that snake. Even the possibility that it might cause problems for her was enough to send her quickly away from it.

Do we treat our temptations that way? Do we flee lest they do us harm? Nope. Far too often, we choose to flirt with them instead of running in the opposite direction. We are convinced that just flirting and dabbling will not do any *real* harm, and then we cross the line and suffer the consequences.

Let us pray today for the wisdom and character to flee from the temptations that pull us away from the Lord who loves us.

Day 56

Persistence

by Jill Holder

James 1:12 "Blessed is the one who endures trials, because when he has stood the test, he will receive the crown that God has promised to those who love Him."

If persistence had a name in our house, it might be "BJ". Our cream-colored tabby cat, BJ, is packed with a steely determination that just won't quit. When he decides that he wants something, nothing will sway him until he gets it.

BJ joined our family after I spoke the infamous last words to my youngest son, Joseph, that we could go into the animal shelter to, "just look, but we can't bring any animals home." On that visit, this little kitten leaned through the cage, put both paws on my son's cheeks without scratching him, looked into his face, and meowed a desperate plea to be set free and join our family. I was true to my claim about going home empty-handed that day. We returned the next morning and brought him home. BJ got what he wanted.

One of the boys had a feathered headband, and BJ became obsessed with a red feather in it. He pulled it out of the headband, so we took it away and put it back. He pulled it out again and again, and each time we replaced it. We hid the headband, thinking the game was over, but BJ found the headband, removed the feather, and ran away with it. Joseph began taking the feather and hiding it around the house for weeks. BJ would roam around for hours, meowing and searching until he found it under a book, on the highest shelf, behind a chest of drawers, or even hidden on the top of a bookcase and under a piece of paper.

Nothing deterred him. He persevered and always found the feather, carrying it around in his mouth until it finally disintegrated into pieces.

As Tim and I were working on our laptops in the kitchen one day, BJ decided that he wanted to jump onto the high kitchen mantle. He meowed and paced back and forth, keeping his focus on the mantle above him. He jumped onto a buffet nearby and gauged the distance. Finding it too far, he paced on the kitchen hearth, still eyeing the mantle, and meowing for what he wanted.

He tried a few more options before he eventually climbed on the back of a wingback chair and launched himself into the air, successfully crossing a distance that we had both thought was insurmountable. He had remained focused and determined, made the jump, achieved the goal, and now sat confidently on the highest perch in the room.

James 1:12 instructs us to persevere in our faith. When the situation is difficult, we are encouraged to not give up. When we are working toward the goal God has set before us, we are instructed to remain focused until the end. If a cat can have extreme persistence in getting adopted, finding a feather, and sitting on a mantle, then surely as people who have instruction from God and place our hope in the Lord, we can follow Him and grow in endurance with the promise of a much greater prize. May we pray today to remain focused and determined. May we pray today for the strength to persevere.

Day 57

God's Will

by Timothy D. Holder

Jeremiah 33:3 "Call to Me, and I will answer you and tell you great and incomprehensible things you do not know."

Hmm, if only it was that easy. If only we could just call to the Lord and have our questions answered. That would be nice. How many times have we prayed for God's direction and only received silence?

I wonder if sometimes we do not hear the answer because we are too busy doing all the talking. Perhaps we are too busy telling God what we want Him to say instead of listening for what He might be telling us.

Sometimes we keep explaining to God that we need guidance on whether to pick Option A or Option B, and it makes us oblivious to His gentle prodding toward Option C.

Sometimes we are busy praying for an answer to our dilemma, and the real answer is that God is nudging us toward just actually praying.

Sometimes God does not answer us right away. He is going to answer us, but before He does, He wants to remind us that He is not here to serve us; we are here to serve Him.

Sometimes we do not hear Him because, even though our prayers are earnest, our sin is great.

Sometimes His temporary silence is not based on any wrong we have done. We do not understand the reason for the waiting, so it allows us to exercise our faith.

If we are faithful and patient in calling out to Him, eventually the answers will come. And sometimes they will be amazing. That said, some answers that might not come in this life at all. Sometimes, the promise made in the Book of Jeremiah might not come to fruition until we see the Lord when we get to heaven. The waiting can be quite hard. The pain of that can be difficult to fathom, much less explain.

Nevertheless, every weight we carry in this life will be worth it in the life to come.

Let us pray today that we would be faithful in calling out to the Lord, even as we wait for the promise to be fulfilled.

Day 58

Shortcuts

by Timothy D. Holder

Matthew 16:24 "Then Jesus said to His disciples, 'If anyone wants to follow after Me, let him deny himself, take up his cross, and follow Me."

As a longtime college professor, I have observed a thing that students do. It is a troubling thing, so I am quite happy that only a small percentage of them are guilty of it. What is their crime? Well, when writing an essay, they copy and paste line after line of someone else's intellectual property.

Instead of a paper based on the students' personal study, discernment, and synthesis of ideas, these students are stealing other people's words and learning little to nothing in the process. Such blatant plagiarism is super easy to catch, of course, so some students think they are taking their deceit to the next level when they randomly go through their paper and trade out some words with synonyms.

The worst example of this was shown to me by a friend at work. A student had changed the word "King" to "Ruler" everywhere it appeared in his paper. The problem was the original word was not in reference to a monarch; it was in reference to the famed civil rights leader.

That's right, dear reader. "Martin Luther King" was referred to as "Martin Luther Ruler" over and over again.

Sigh...

Of course, the point here—and I think you can see it coming—is what about us when it comes to our spiritual lives? Do we take lazy shortcuts? Are we focused on being disciples, or do we go to extremes to avoid being serious students and ambassadors of our faith? Are we involved in some ministry inside or outside of church where we are just pretending to put in some effort, but we are not really committed to doing the hard work that ministries require?

The academic shortcut I described above is not good for student learning or success. In a similar way, spiritual shortcuts are not good for our spiritual growth. Let us pray today that we would live out the Lord's commands for discipleship with integrity.

Day 59

Role Modeling

by Jill Holder

Matthew 18:6 "But whoever causes one of these little ones who believe in Me to fall away—it would be better for him if a heavy millstone were hung around his neck, and he were drowned in the depths of the sea."

One of the greatest joys of my life has been teaching my students in the classroom. As most experienced teachers know, it can often be a mentally and physically exhausting job of wearing multiple hats all day followed by evenings, weekends, and summers used to prepare for future lessons. However, it is worth it all to have the opportunity to make a difference in the life of a child.

Because I am no longer in the classroom full-time, I especially enjoy jumping back in as a substitute teacher when my acting career allows. Recently, I was asked to sub in a third-grade classroom at the school where I had taught before and my youngest boys still attend. As I walked into the classroom to relieve the teacher's aide that morning, the students ran to embrace me in a big group hug with shouts of, "Ms. Martin! We hoped it would be you! We love you!" Wow! What a special way to start my day! Don't we all wish every day could start like this?

As the students settled down in their seats and we began to go over the morning work, one girl raised her hand and said, "Ms. Martin, I saw you at the park the other day." Not to be outdone, a boy in the back said, "Well, I saw her in line buying books at the bookstore!" Another child spoke up and claimed that he had seen me eating at a local restaurant. Next, a student said that she was seated near me at a band concert. Two more said that they had walked behind me at an art show. Every single place they named was somewhere that Tim and I had been together recently. While we enjoyed being together around town on dates, laughing and talking, we had no idea that the children were watching us.

In a previous devotion, there was a reminder that we are setting an example for our peers as we seek to reflect Christ in our daily lives. We probably also realize that our own children are watching us as they form opinions on what it means to follow God. But let us not forget that our actions are also impacting other children in our world. May we pray to be more aware of this and live lives that point them to the Lord.

Day 60

Friends

by Timothy D. Holder

Proverbs 13:20 "The one who walks with the wise will become wise, but a companion of fools will suffer harm."

One can find a whole lot of articles and blogs on the internet regarding how to be successful. There are many formulas, plans, and paradigms that, the writers say, can turn your life around and help you achieve your dreams.

Interestingly, I was reading one such article today that offered four keys to success, and number one on the list dealt with friendship. The premise was that if we choose friends who are better than us, they will raise us up to their standards. And the inverse is also true: If we associate with, for example, slackers, we stand a good chance of, um, slacking.

Of course, there is an obvious flaw in only associating with those who are our betters: If they are driven by the same standard, they will not want to hang out with us.

Setting that aside, the writer makes a great point. I have long benefited from cultivating relationships with people who possess traits I admire.

Unfortunately, I have seen the opposite at work too. Years ago, I taught dual enrollment courses, which meant I would offer college courses on a high school campus to high school students. In one of my classes, I had a student who was unfocused and disinterested. He did not take his education very seriously, but he was smart enough that he still made good grades.

Another thing about this guy was that he was clearly the alpha in his friend group. Oftentimes, he led his friends off task. They did not possess his intellectual gifts, however, and they struggled (sometimes unsuccessfully) to make decent grades. He led them downhill with his attitude and behavior, but he was smart enough to avoid the consequences personally.

What about us? Do we have Christians in our lives who help us grow in our faith and leadership, do we associate with people who drag us in the opposite direction, or is our peer group meandering along in mediocrity? May we pray today that we would cultivate relationships with people who bring out our best, and may we take a long hard look at those who don't. And may we strive to help bring out the best in others.

Day 61

Animals

by Timothy D. Holder

Job 1:8 "Then the Lord said to Satan, 'Have you considered My servant Job? No one else on earth is like him, a man of perfect integrity, who fears God and turns away from evil.'"

People can be pretty proud of their pets. It gets a little unreal sometimes.

Person One: My dog can open the back door all by himself when he needs to go outside.
Person Two: My dog responds to twenty-seven distinct voice commands.
Person Three: My dog can play the violin. He's not even classically trained—he just plays by ear, and it is absolutely beautiful.

I like animals just fine.
All right, full disclosure: People who are connected with me on social media know I am obsessed with apes. But I am really only interested in fake movie apes and pictures of chimps. I would never want to be around apes in real life. They can be dangerous.
Anyway, one of the interesting things about dating Jill is I discovered she has six animals—two dogs, two cats, and two horses. This has been quite educational for me. I have learned a lot about the material and emotional needs of pets. The animal I have connected with the most is BJ the cat, who was the subject of Jill's devotional on Day 56.
BJ is just fascinating. Sometimes, he acts like he truly loves me. He is content to be held, or he will sit in my

lap and want to be petted. At other times, he wants attention, but he is totally selfish about it, like when I am typing on my laptop, and BJ walks onto the keys and lies down.

There are times when he ignores me altogether.

And then there are the times when he jumps up on tables and counters. When we tell him to get down, he sometimes ignores us, but at other times he will look at us. And then he ignores us. When scooped off the table or counter, he might meow once in protest. He is not really angry; it is more like simple back talk.

Oftentimes, he will jump back up there again almost immediately. It is not that he forgets he is being bad; he just does not seem to care.

In the Old Testament, Job was a servant of the Lord who tried to live a righteous life. In contrast, there is nothing particularly righteous about BJ. He just does whatever he feels like doing.

What about us? Are we more like Job or BJ? Do we strive to live a righteous life, or do we actually just go out and do whatever feels good and natural in the moment—indulging our passions and selfishness and satisfying our animal nature?

We usually only think of Job when we think of suffering. May we prayerfully consider his example today as a man who tried to please the Lord. May we strive to live up to that example today.

Day 62

Illusions

by Timothy D. Holder

James 5:16 "Therefore, confess your sins to one another and pray for one another, so that you may be healed. The prayer of a righteous person is very powerful in its effect."

I knew a guy when I was a college student, and I will refer to him as "Glenn." This is not one of those instances where I have to change his name to safeguard his reputation or protect myself from being sued; it is just a story about Glenn Record.

I was always impressed by my friend Glenn. He was smart, good looking, and an easy conversationalist. One time I walked into Glenn's dorm room at the beginning of a new term, and I quickly noticed that he had a picture of a strikingly attractive young woman on his desk. There were a few other guys in the room with us, and we began asking Glenn about the picture.

He said he discovered her over the break. He told us he saw her for the first time at a mall and things rapidly progressed.

We were happy for Glenn. We were impressed.

But then he told us the truth.

He had simply bought a picture frame as it was, and he did not put a new picture in it. The young woman was the model whose picture was already in the frame. He really did see her (picture) for the first time at a mall.

Glenn was amused by his deception, and so were we, but imagine if he had not told us the truth. How long might we have been fooled? Possibly, Glenn could have maintained his ruse for quite some time since his hometown was in a different state than our school was.

Glenn's deception was funny and harmless, nothing more, but what about our deceptions? Is our reality—our thought life, our internet viewing habits, our private behaviors, our spiritual disciplines—something different than what the world sees?

Let us pray today that if we are pretending our reality is prettier than it really is, we would repent of such deception. Maybe some of us need to make the choice today "to confess our sins, one to the other."

Day 63

Unity

by Jill Holder

Philippians 2:2 "Make my joy complete by thinking the same way, having the same love, united in spirit, intent on one purpose."

When my children were younger, I had the great wish as a mother to take a picture of all five of them one Easter in their new church clothes, looking nice, smiling, and happy all at the same time. Lots of preparation was put into choosing coordinating clothing, getting all of them dressed with hair combed just right, setting up the camera on a tripod, posing them in front of the nicest flowers by the pasture, and attempting to take the shot. The wildcard to getting the picture to turn out right was to keep everyone looking nice until I could snap the shot.

Joseph, my youngest, was two years old and full of adventure. Even though he was typically covered in dirt, food, or any messy substance he could find within moments of getting dressed each day, I somehow made the insane choice to dress him in a little white organza shirt with white silk trim on the collar and matching organza shorts. He wore white knee socks and white dress shoes, and he was totally adorable. Alas, all good things must come to an end, and his neat and clean appearance ended all too soon.

Knowing that the older kids could stay posed the longest, I waited until the last minute to pop Joseph into the picture. When I turned around to get him, he was gone. I still remember that sinking feeling of realizing that he was definitely getting filthy somewhere. We looked around, and then saw the soles of two previously white toddler dress shoes sticking out from under the bushes and weeds at the edge of the pasture. I pulled him out by his ankles as he protested every inch of the way. His clothes were muddy, his socks were stained, and my vision of clean kids in a sweet picture went up in smoke before my eyes. It turns out, he was intent on chasing a rabbit.

Joseph is fourteen years old now, and he still remembers that moment with frustration toward me for interrupting his exploits. He had seen a rabbit run into the bushes, had the thought that he had never petted a live rabbit before, and had one purpose that day; he was going to catch that rabbit! I had a different purpose altogether, of course. I wanted a family picture with clean kids. We were pulling in different directions, and as a result, neither of us achieved what we had hoped. After I cleaned him up as best as I could that day, we talked and made a plan. We would take the picture quickly with his siblings and then change him into play clothes and go exploring together. We now had a united purpose, and the new plan went off without a hitch.

How often are we "chasing rabbits" when someone else has the purpose of "taking the picture"? In our Scripture for today, we are encouraged to be of the same mind, united in spirit and purpose. The ultimate example has been shown to us through the unity of purpose shared by God with His Son, Jesus. There are many examples in Scripture that tell how Jesus communicated with the Father often through prayer, such as in Luke 6:12, Luke 9:18, and Luke 9:29. They talked.

But they didn't just communicate; they also had a unified goal: to bring salvation to the world. It was a big plan with a massive goal, and it was accomplished with unity of purpose. Let us pray today to be people who strive for unity of purpose in our relationships, work, and homes, and in bringing others to the Lord through communication and achieving unity together.

Day 64

Goals

by Timothy D. Holder

Psalm 127:1 "Unless the Lord builds a house, its builders labor over it in vain; unless the Lord watches over a city, the watchman stays alert in vain."

When I was a little kid, my brother John and I used to fight a lot. One time we went at it in the naval base grocery store in Charleston, South Carolina, where my dad was stationed. He was stationed at the base, not the grocery store, which is significant only insofar as he was not there when John and I started fighting, and my mother was not looking at us. An elderly man who was shopping nearby had to break us up.

Since our fight that day was interrupted, I will always look on it as a draw, and I feel pretty good about that. I mean, my mother was mortified, but we can't all be happy, right?

The reason I was so pleased with my stalemate that day is because John invariably beat me. He was older, slightly bigger, meaner, and definitely tougher than me.

At one point I was in a phase where I would cry after we fought. I do not think it was solely because he dished out so much pain. I believe there was also some angst that we were even fighting in the first place—that things were so bad that this was how we needed to resolve them.

One day there was a different end to the story. A staple of action TV shows of the 1960s and 1970s was the fight scenes, and I really enjoyed them. It was not that I would see a guy get beat up on TV and then want to go fight my classmates. Rather, I was fascinated by the physicality of it. I think I liked the art part of the martial arts. And it was interesting to me since I was small for my age that oftentimes the hero could win against opponents who were bigger, or the star would come out on top even when he was fighting multiple bad guys.

Anyway, there was a move that was commonly used back then where the hero would be on his back on the ground, the bad guy would jump on him, the hero would get his feet under the villain, and then the hero would push the bad guy away.

So, one day John and I were fighting in the laundry room, and I became convinced I could execute this move against him. John got me down pretty quickly, I got my feet under him, and…

It worked to perfection!

Not only was I able to push John off me with my feet, but my maneuver also ended the fight. When John went backward, he fell into some roller skates or something and hurt his arm a little bit. He was fine, really, but it hurt him enough that it made him cry, and he did not want to fight anymore.

Let me again make clear, this was not a typical ending to one of our fights.

I got sent to my room, and once I was alone there, I could feel myself getting emotional. I remember saying out loud, "I am not going to cry. I won."

And then I cried.

It was frustrating. I had a problem (John was winning all our fights). I came up with a plan, and I executed it. I thought that finally beating John would make me happy, but it did not. My real problem was not that my brother was working me over; it was that I was fighting with my brother. I accomplished my goal (of winning one single fight out of many), but it was the wrong goal.

What kinds of goals are we pursuing these days? Are they selfish? Maybe they are not bad in and of themselves, but perhaps they are not worthy of our time. Let us pray today that God would put worthwhile goals on our hearts.

    PS: Nowadays, John is a good and sometimes great brother.
    PPS: That move I executed really was awesome. I wish I had a digital copy of it so I could send it to John periodically.

Day 65

Discernment

by Elissa Keck Hodge

Philippians 1:9-11 "And it is my prayer that your love may abound more and more, with knowledge and all discernment, so that you may approve what is excellent, and so be pure and blameless for the day of Christ, filled with the fruit of righteousness that comes through Jesus Christ, to the glory and praise of God."

One of the greatest joys of parenting is seeing and experiencing the world through the eyes of one's children. I love hearing my children's explanations or interpretations of stories or events. For example, one day my son (at age four) brought home a journal from school dated April 1st. He had written the numeral four all over the page, dozens and dozens of times. I asked him what this meant. He said, "That day was 'April Four's Day,' and my teacher asked us to draw or write something that represented this day." I laughed as I realized he heard "April Four's" instead of "April Fool's." I'm sure he heard his teacher say "April Fool's Day" a number of times throughout the day, but since he had no reference for the day, he responded to what he *thought* he heard.

And then there was the time my other son was singing the tune of the familiar children's song "Hot Cross Buns" to the following text:

Hotdog buns, hotdog buns
Give them to your daughters
Give them to your sons
One a penny, two a penny
Hotdog buns

Here is the original text for reference:

Hot cross buns, hot cross buns
Give them to your daughters
Give them to your sons
One a penny, two a penny
Hot cross buns

    In his mind he *thought* he was singing the correct text—it sounded right. And, after all, why wouldn't you give hotdog buns to your daughters and sons? Makes sense—at least to him.

    While these events were funny and cute, I realize that they sang or drew what they heard. It was close to the real thing but missed the mark because my boys hadn't learned the true phrase or text. How many times are we close? *Almost* right? I've often heard discernment defined as "the difference between right and almost right." What are the consequences of being *almost* right? What does this mean if we are almost right in our faith, our understanding of who God is, or our understanding of how we are to live and love those around us? These consequences are eternal. How do we know what's right or true? We go to the source. We study, meditate, and hunger after God's Word. We don't rely on what we hear in the world. We can only recognize truth by studying truth. And when we do so, we receive wisdom and discernment "so that we may approve what is excellent, and so be pure and blameless for the day of Christ, filled with the fruit of righteousness that comes through Jesus Christ, to the glory and praise of God."

Day 66

Change

by Jill Holder

Ecclesiastes 3:11A "He has made everything appropriate in its time."

If you know me at all, you know I love flowers. To me, flowers make the world a better place just by doing what they were intended to do: grow and bloom. One of my favorite pastimes in spring through fall is to head to my favorite plant nursery, walk through the rows of flowers, and choose a few new favorites to bring home, plant, and nurture. I personally believe that every flower is a miracle; you can never have too many! My favorite memory from my last birthday is when I opened my front door to find Tim standing on my porch, holding out a beautiful bouquet of pink roses for me as a gift. Priceless!

Many years ago, when I was creating the flower beds outside my new home, I planted a row of crepe myrtle bushes along the end of the house. Each year, the bushes would fill with beautiful clusters of pink flowers. The children and I enjoyed how pretty they were outside, and I often brought the blooms inside for cut flower arrangements to brighten the kitchen table. And, every year, the bushes grew more and more.

Eventually, the bushes dwarfed some of the surrounding trees. They became taller than the house and still kept growing. The branches spread until they began to cover the roof of the garage. My dad noticed that they were actually beginning to damage the roof shingles. He brought it to my attention and suggested that I cut them down, but I wouldn't hear of it. I loved those bushes and their pink blooms, so I held onto keeping them, and the damage continued.

The next spring, Dad mentioned it again, and I still refused. The trees were healthy, beautiful, and I had enjoyed them for years, not wanting to let them go. By the third spring, I couldn't ignore the damage any longer. I finally agreed that the time for the towering bushes to damage the house had to come to an end. Although they were beautiful, I enjoyed them, and I had held on to them for as long as I could, I had to let them go. So down they came.

Just like the crepe myrtle bushes, how many things are we holding on to in our lives that God once placed there as good for a season, yet the season has passed? Is it a volunteer position, a job, an activity, or a friendship that has turned toxic that we need to release? Let us examine our lives today and pray to let go of those things that were brought into our lives for a season that has passed.

One other thing to note: A few months after the bushes were cut down, new growth began to sprout forth from the roots that will be producing new flowers by next year. Moving forward is often needed to find the miracles that God has planned for our new season of life.

Day 67

Repetition

by Timothy D. Holder

Galatians 6:14-15 "But as for me, I will never boast about anything except the cross of our Lord Jesus Christ. The world has been crucified to me through the cross, and I to the world. For both circumcision and uncircumcision mean nothing; what matters instead is a new creation."

If you were to read the Book of Galatians, you would find that Paul talks about how our salvation comes from the work of Christ, not our own efforts. One of the interesting things about how Paul handles this is the fact that he returns to the same theme in all six chapters of the book.

Why did Paul keep writing it?

Because we need to keep reading it and hearing it.

One time when I was twenty-eight years old and sitting in a Sunday School class, the teacher talked about how we needed to reach out to people and be more relational.

I went to a different class the next week, but not because I was offended by the message. The class I had been in was for twentysomethings, which fit me, but over time just about all of them were married or engaged. I was not even dating anybody, and I just felt like at that point in my life with that particular group and my personality, I might need to go to a different class if I wanted to develop better connections with people.

Anyway, that next week, I started in a new class, and it was for singles. The age range was so wide—both older and younger—that it did not feel like a good fit for me. But interestingly, the teacher talked about how we all needed to reach out to people if the class was going to grow.

A week later, I visited some friends in St. Louis. At church that Sunday, the pastor talked about how much it meant to him when he was going through a health situation and many people in the church were especially kind to him.

One more week passed, and I was back in Kentucky. I decided to visit a new church, and the pastor talked about the importance of Christians being friendly.

On the fifth week, I returned to the church I visited a week before, and I went to a Sunday School class. There was an emphasis that week on the importance of going out of our way to speak to one another.

For five weeks in a row, I had gotten varieties of the same message: We need to be nicer to people than we are comfortable being. This was an important message for me because I was shy. My attitude was that if someone was nice to me, I would be nice back. But if they ignored me, I was comfortable ignoring them too.

After hearing the same message for five weeks in a row, I began to see the flaw in my thinking: If I were seated next to shy people, none of us would ever reach out.

Sometimes we need to hear the same message over and over for it to really sink in. Maybe we need to be reminded of God's grace; maybe we need to be reminded to show grace to others. Let us pray today that we would notice what God has been telling us over and over. And let us pray that we would be changed by the revelation.

Day 68

Blessings

by Timothy D. Holder

Psalm 103:2 "My soul, bless the Lord, and do not forget all His benefits."

Sometimes I have breakfast with Matt Huckaba. As I write this, Matt is twenty-three and I am fifty-four. I first got to know him when he was a college student, and we have kept in touch ever since. One thing I pondered, as we had breakfast recently, was how he had maintained relationships with friends of his who had different majors, moved out of state, gotten married before him, or stayed single after he got married. Matt has also done a good job of staying connected with me, even as my life has gotten busy and I have been pulled in many directions. in short, Matt is quite relational.

I was thinking, as I drove away from our most recent breakfast, that Matt models good friendship skills. He is open about his life and his feelings, he takes an interest in his friends' lives, and he regularly touches base with people. He has a variety of interesting, um, interests, which is a trait that keeps his conversations with me stimulating.

The point is that Matt's friendship is a blessing to me and being around someone with his relational skills is part of that blessing. I like associating with people I can learn from.

I am grateful to God that I have great role models in so many areas of my life.

It is easy to fall into the habit of complaining about the things that frustrate us, but we would do well to consider our blessings. We all have our Matt Huckabas of one sort or another. Let us pray today prayers of thanks for the fact that we get more blessings than we deserve.

Day 69

Priorities

by Jill Holder

Colossians 3:2 "Set your minds on things above, not on earthly things."

As an actress, I routinely travel out of town for film projects. Sometimes things go exactly as planned, but at other times even the best-laid plans can go awry.

During the national gasoline shortage in the summer of 2021, I had to travel out of state for a couple of days for an acting role. To be prepared, I checked the gasoline supply in advance online and contacted a friend that had driven through the area just the day before. Both sources confirmed that the shortage had not hit that area yet, so I filled up my car on the way out of town and headed to the studio. I stopped along the way to top off the tank as well. Although I used up most of the gas by the time I arrived at my destination, I noticed several gas stations near the studio that were open with cars parked at all the pumps. I was totally fine!

After a late wardrobe fitting, I walked to my car with the last employee still on the lot to find that my cell phone was dead because my charging cord had stopped working. No problem. I could replace that, right? I drove to the gas station to grab a new cord and fill up my almost empty tank, only to find that the station had no more charging cords for sale and NO GASOLINE. It seems that the cars at the pumps were parked there in the hope that they could be first in line when the gas trucks came in the next few days. In fact, the attendant informed me, there was no gasoline for miles around, and she recommended that I avoid the only hotel in town if I valued my safety. Perfect.

With one mile of gasoline remaining in the tank, I found a grocery store that had a phone charger. I purchased it, plugged in my phone just enough to get it turned on, and sent Tim a quick message to let him know that now was probably a really great time to pray. I began to realize that when my car ran out of gas, I would no longer be able to recharge my cell phone. But I had my laptop as well! I turned off the car to save fuel and plugged the phone cord into my laptop to continue charging it. In less than a minute, the laptop died. And then the phone died again.

The only option I could think of at this point was to turn on the car to charge the phone as much as possible while I used my last mile of gasoline to try to get to a safer place. Otherwise, it was a night alone in my car in a sketchy area with no way to even call for help. I prayed, knew Tim was praying, continued to pray, and headed down the road.

Stopping at a traffic light, I looked up in amazement at the welcome sight of a gasoline tanker truck pulling into a gas station across the road to refill the pumps! Praise God! I quickly turned around and followed him into the station along with most of the cars on the road. Cars and trucks quickly lined up across the parking lot and far down the street, blocking all traffic in both directions, waiting while the driver pumped the gasoline from his truck into the supply tanks. Our cars were turned off and windows down in the heat to conserve what gasoline we each had left. Eventually, the first few cars in line were able to begin fueling their cars, and I was relieved. I could get gas, turn on my car, charge my phone, and call Tim, who was actually preparing to make the long drive to bring me a can of gasoline and make sure that I was safe. Now I could drive myself to a nice hotel across town where I could eat, sleep, and be close to the next day's film set.

And then the pumps jammed. All the gasoline pumps stopped working. The lady gas attendant began going down the multiple lines of cars, speaking to each driver. When she came to my car, she told me that I would have to leave for the night, that the pumps would be reset the following morning at 5:00 AM, and that I could come back then. Letting her know a bit about my fuel situation, I asked her if I could at least spend the night in my car at the pump. She warned me that I might not be safe but that I could park there if I wanted to risk it. She then asked me why I was in town. I simply said that I am an actress and had to be there for a film project that day, but I had to be on set in a new location the following morning. She then emphatically said, "That's important! I'm going to help you!" And she did. After the parking lot eventually cleared, she motioned me up to the pump, reset the system, and let me purchase enough gasoline to get a hundred and fifty miles down the road that night.

Was I grateful? Absolutely! But her reasoning for helping me blew my mind. It was not that I was a woman traveling alone with less than a mile left before I was stranded with no gasoline. It wasn't that I would be spending the night in my car in an unsafe area. It wasn't even that I would not have a working cell phone to call for help in the event of an emergency. It was simply that, to her, my job as an actress was more important than those things. I can certainly say that's not what I was thinking!

But how often is our mindset focused on things that are of less importance? How often do we place our priorities on the things of this world instead of on things of eternal significance? Do we place greater value in possessions, fame, or success than we place on people, caring for others as Christ taught, and sharing about their eternal importance to God? Let us pray today to train our minds to focus on what is eternal and align our values with God's priority list.

Day 70

Surprises

by Timothy D. Holder

James 1:3 "…because you know that the testing of your faith produces endurance."

I have been in several weddings throughout my adult life, and usually nothing quirky happens to me there, but there was this one time…

The setup for this particular bridal party was not the standard "men on one side, women on the other." In this instance, the men and women were paired off and stood on both sides of the bride and groom. It is a placement system that is not often used, but there is certainly nothing wrong with it, so my spot on the platform was not the quirky part of the story.

I noticed shortly before the ceremony started that the woman next to me gave her young daughter a cough drop. I was not really paying attention to what happened next, but I wish I had been. A few minutes later, I was standing on the platform, the ceremony had already started, and the woman turned to me and whispered, "Put this in your pocket. I don't have pockets in my dress."

It was the cough drop.
It was wet and sticky.
I was not enthusiastic about having a partially used cough drop in my hand, but I did not want to put it in my rented tuxedo. That just seemed like an unkind "gift" for the employee at the tuxedo shop.

The ceremony proceeded, and at one point the bride had to lift her veil or something, I guess. (It happened several years ago, and what the bride was doing was not burned into my memory.) Anyway, she handed her bouquet to the woman standing next to me. But the bride struggled with her task a little bit more, even with her hands freed up. The woman next to me decided to help her, so I was handed the bouquet.

For those readers who are keeping score, I was standing on the platform in the middle of a wedding ceremony, holding the bridal bouquet and a sticky cough drop.

I did not learn until after the ceremony was over that, in fact, the cough drop was not partially used. It was just wet and sticky because the bridesmaid had been holding it tightly in her hand after her daughter rejected it. At least that is what the woman told me.

As we go through life, we experience surprises. Some are fantastic, and some go quite far in the other direction. I have heard wise people say that God is never surprised. Our unexpected circumstances might throw us for a loop, but God is never caught off-guard. Let us pray today that we will still trust in God, even when our world gets weird. Sometimes life hands us things that are worse than sticky cough drops and wedding bouquets. Even then, let us pray for the faith to still trust in God.

Day 71

Titles

by Timothy D. Holder

Acts 11:26C "The disciples were first called Christians at Antioch."

When I was ordained into the ministry in October 2017, it was a special thing for me. It still is. I am honored to have been given the title of "reverend." It has, however, prompted a question on occasion. Every so often, I will be asked, "Is it 'Reverend Doctor Holder,' or 'Doctor Reverend Holder'?"

In case you are wondering, dear reader, I believe the appropriate title is "reverend doctor." I did not bother to look it up because I do not want it to be that important to me.

I am also sometimes asked if I would rather be called "doctor," "reverend," or both. I always say it depends on the circumstances. If I am performing a religious function, like preaching a sermon or officiating a wedding, I would prefer the title "reverend" (if a title is needed). If I am involved in a public speaking venue and talking about presidents, or if I am in a formal academic setting, "doctor" makes more sense. I never expect to be called by both.

While my friends and acquaintances are familiar with those two titles for me, there is a third I will occasionally invoke: I am a Kentucky colonel. Or maybe I used to be a Kentucky colonel—I do not know what the statute of limitations is on that. What does it mean to be a Kentucky colonel? I was told that it used to mean you were a guy whom the governor of Kentucky could call on in difficult times. What does that mean? I do not know. By the time I was notified that I was one, it just meant I was invited once a year to a barbeque fundraiser.

Some titles mean more than others. Some titles are taken seriously, and others are not. Does the adulterer take the title of "spouse" seriously? I would say no.

What about the title of "Christian"? Do we feel the weight of that? Are we inspired to live up to it, or do we take it for granted? Do we think about the responsibilities of that title, or do we just focus on the benefits? Our actions and attitudes matter. There are people watching us who recognize that we wear that title. What are they seeing when they look at us?

Let us pray today that we would take the title of "Christian" as a sacred thing. Let us pray that we would be worthy of the name today.

Day 72

Feelings

by Timothy D. Holder

Galatians 5:22-23 "But the fruit of the Spirit is love, joy, peace, patience, kindness, goodness, gentleness, and self-control. The law is not against such things."

When I was a kid, I lived in Central Florida. My favorite NFL team was Washington, but the closest team geographically was the Tampa Bay Buccaneers. When the Bucs first entered the league, they were historically bad (they lost their first 26 regular season games in a row), but I developed something of an interest in them because they were kind of local. They were on TV and in the newspapers a lot, so I got to know who the players were, and it made me kind of care about them.

One year, they played a preseason game in Orlando, and my dad took my brothers and me to watch them. I had never been to an NFL game before, so even though it was just the preseason, it was pretty cool. The Bucs were playing the Atlanta Falcons, and the game was competitive because neither of them were very good at the time.

Since it was a preseason game, the outcome was meaningless, but not to me. I wanted to see the Bucs win. Because the game was close, and at times the Bucs had the upper hand, I really thought they were going to pull it out. But toward the end, the game started slipping away from them.

It was getting late, and my dad was concerned about traffic. When it became clear that the Bucs no longer had a chance, my dad pulled the plug and said it was time to go.

I was really frustrated that a potential win had turned into a probable loss, and then I was upset that I had to leave my one and only in-person football game.

I complained…um…energetically.

I had no control over the game, of course, so I focused my complaints on leaving early. My poor dad had sacrificed hours of his time and a not insignificant amount of money, and this was how the evening was going to end—with me complaining all the way to the car and then some.

I was whining about a thing. But the thing I was complaining about was not the real problem. It was not my dad's fault that the Falcons showed some surprising grit in the fourth quarter.

How often are we guilty of this behavior? How often do we lash out at someone when we are frustrated about something unrelated? Even though I was a kid, it did not make it okay that I was taking out my frustration on those around me. How much worse is it, though, when some of us do this even as adults? If we tend to lash out at others when we are upset, stressed, or sad, let us pray today that we would not be so selfish. And if we are on the receiving end of such behavior, let us pray for the fortitude to set up boundaries, but let us also pray for a measure of grace.

Day 73

God's Love

by Jill Holder

Ephesians 2:4-5 "But God, who is rich in mercy, because of His great love for us, made us alive with Christ even though we were dead in trespasses. You are saved by grace!"

My children have been blessed to have many amazing, loving teachers over the years who have not only taught them intellectually, but also taught them by example of the miraculous love of God. One of those teachers was Ann Roback.

Two of my sons were privileged to have Mrs. Roback as a kindergarten teacher. The oldest of the two, Joshua, was a very engaging and expressive little guy with a mind and heart so full of thoughts that he couldn't contain them. Literally, none of them. His report card often had a glowing list of comments followed by the word "talkative."

As we walked through the school parking lot to our car after school early in the year, he confessed that he had not had his very best day. According to him, as he and many of his classmates had gone through their day, they had spent more time talking than following directions and had forfeited some classroom privileges as a result of their choices. As a teacher myself, I sympathized with Mrs. Roback much more than with her students, and I commented that I was sure that the classroom behavior had made it a difficult day for his teacher. He said, "Oh, no, Mom! Mrs. Roback is fine. She told us that even though she might get disappointed in our choices, she always loves us!" So, when the next morning came, Josh happily jumped out of the car and ran to class and his teacher, secure in the knowledge that she loved him despite his behavior from the day before.

Isn't that a beautiful picture of how God loves us? There are certainly days, weeks, and even seasons in our lives when we can acknowledge that we have not made the best choices. Maybe we have become so busy that we have pushed God to the side until the day when things slow down; possibly we have been hurtful to others or have allowed anger to get the best of us. We might have chosen to follow a path that had devastating consequences for ourselves and others.

However, even on the worst of days when our choices are abominable, God still loves us. He may be disappointed in our choices, but He still loves us with open arms. The evidence of this love is this: Even when we were sinners and very imperfect people who were not following Him, He still chose to sacrifice His Son for us.

So, just as Josh ran to his teacher after a day of talking out of turn, we can still run to God when we have behaved at our worst because we can be secure in His love for us no matter our actions. May we pray today to embrace His great love for us.

Day 74

Excuses

by Timothy D. Holder

John 15:22 "If I had not come and spoken to them, they would not be guilty of sin. Now they have no excuse for their sin."

It was early on a Saturday morning, and they were taking security seriously at the Orlando International Airport. The line was starting to back up where passengers empty their pockets and take off their shoes for the security scans. I had not quite reached that point in the process when a minor incident occurred.

In anticipation of a lot of passengers coming along soon, security had set up barriers that forced a person to walk from one side to the other, back and forth, slowly moving forward to the scanning area. As a customer, it was a little tedious to take all those extra steps, but it was easier to set up the lanes before the huge crowds got there, so it made sense.

I had made my way about two-thirds through the winding route when a security guard looked in my general direction and bellowed, "Sir! Please don't do that!"

I looked over my shoulder and saw a guy who clearly did not feel like walking from one side of the area to the other over and over again. He was unhooking each barrier, stepping forward and securing it back again behind himself as he moved forward.

When the security guard called him out, the man stopped what he was doing, but he grumbled, "Security gonna make me miss my flight."

The man's complaint was absurd. Even if there had been no barriers at all, he still would have had to wait just as long once he reached the scanning area, so his efforts to save steps did not buy him any time; they just demonstrated that he was too lazy to walk through the route as it was intended.

It was interesting that he even bothered to mutter such a lame excuse. But it leaves me wondering how often we do that with our sins. We gossip, and we say we are just telling the truth. We say or do something hurtful to someone, and we say they deserve it because they hurt us first, as if the Bible ever justified a Christian rationalizing such a thing that way. We sin, and we justify it based on someone else doing something worse.

We can be better than that. We are called to be better than that. Let us pray today that instead of making unconvincing arguments to justify wrong behavior, we would choose to behave honorably before the Lord.

Day 75

Discipline

by Timothy D. Holder

Colossians 2:18 "Let no one condemn you by delighting in ascetic practices and the worship of angels, claiming access to a visionary realm. Such people are inflated by empty notions of their unspiritual mind."

Several years ago, I read that the key to success as a blogger was to be consistent. If you release your content at the same time each week, your readers will begin to look forward to it. They will be able to count on you.

In response to that, I published something weekly for years. My goal was to attract people to my writing so that when I had a book come out, they would want to buy it.

It did not work.

There was not an appreciable gain in book sales that resulted from my blogging. I was putting the work in. I was disciplined and faithful in my commitment to the task, but it was not making a difference. The idea was logical, but the result was disappointing.

More recently, I listened to a talk from a career military guy who was extolling the virtues of making one's bed every day. To me, that seemed like a waste of time. You are just going to get back in the bed every night, so why take the effort to straighten up the blankets, pillows, and sheets? It sounded like discipline for the sake of discipline. It seemed pointless.

The old sailor argued, though, that making your bed helps establish a mindset for the day. If you make your bed after you get up in the morning, you have already successfully completed your first task. One could also argue that you are establishing the precedent of leaving things better than you found them. And it makes it a little harder to rationalize slipping right back into the bed, so it pushes you forward and toward productivity.

So, I have started making my bed.

Thus, at one time I thought consistent blogging was a meaningful act of discipline and bedmaking was a useless one. But after reflection, I now see both in the opposite light.

What about the disciplines we engage in as believers? Are we faithfully adhering to standards that are good for our souls and make a positive difference in the lives of those around us, or have we committed ourselves to some practices and mindsets that really do not have lasting value? Perhaps we have contented ourselves with comfortable routines and called them "disciplines." We can be better than that.

Let us pray today for the wisdom to be discerning about the disciplines we practice. May we cast off that which has no value and redouble our efforts at those things that do.

Day 76

Service

by Jill Holder

1 Corinthians 12:5-6 "There are different ministries, but the same Lord. And there are different activities, but the same God works all of them in each person."

When my five children were younger, we decided to run a race together. I was already scheduled to run a half marathon at Disney World, so when the opportunity came for us to run a 5K together the preceding morning, we jumped at it. Honestly, what could be more magical than running together as a family in sunny Florida at the happiest place on earth?

The morning of the race, we got up super early, dressed, and arrived at the starting gate with water bottles in hand and racing numbers pinned to our shirts well before the sunrise. We would be running the race in Epcot, beginning at a side entrance, running around the lake in World Showcase, then on to the big ball of Spaceship Earth and out to the main entrance of the park. Disney employees and characters would be along the route, waving and cheering us on to the finish line.

Just before the race began, my oldest son, who was the most experienced runner in the family, stepped up beside me, gave me a look, and said, "So, do we have to stay together for this whole race?" I smiled, told him to go ahead, and did not see him again until after I crossed the finish line. He had gone to the head of the crowd of over 5,000 people with a seriously competitive expression. He wound up finishing in sixth place.

My daughter, the oldest, ran close to me and helped her younger brothers. She encouraged them, helped them stay safe, and enjoyed the humorous moments that come with being around kids. We laughed a lot that day!

My middle kid, the most outgoing guy who loves people, started off with us, but his long legs quickly helped him leave us behind. Multiple times I caught sight of him across the lake from us, laughing and smiling as he ran and talked with different groups of strangers. At the end of the race, he remarked that the highlight of the morning was having the chance to meet so many new people.

My fourth child, a boy, ran in spurts. He would yell, "Burst of speed!", bolt up ahead for a minute, and then slowly jog, panting, as he built up the strength to do the same thing again. Since my daughter was often holding his hand, her sore arm was the victim of this running technique. His last burst of speed propelled him over the finish line.

The youngest child rode in the stroller, with me pushing him most of the way. If you have never tried to run full out while pushing an umbrella stroller, I have some advice: Don't! As he rode along, drinking cold drinks from his sippy cup, he occasionally looked behind him and yelled out to his family and strangers alike, "Hurry up, slowpoke!" He was clearly not winning any friends along the way. Given the choice to get out of the stroller and run across the finish line or ride across it, he sat right where he was and raised his hands in the air as he rolled across.

The thing is, although we all ran the race differently, we all finished. Some of us ran ahead and finished more quickly, some ran in the middle and met new friends, and some stayed back and helped the younger boys make it to the end. But we all finished.

This is similar to how we work for the Lord in life. With the exception of my littlest guy, who gets a pass because he was only three years old, we all had a good goal in mind, and we all achieved it honorably. However, none of us worked in the same way to accomplish the goal. As we work with others in our homes, churches, and jobs, may we remember that we may have different ways of working, but we serve the same God who is at work in each of us.

Let us pray today that we would be sensitive to others who share our goal of working for the Lord but may have different—yet equally honorable—ways of serving Him.

Day 77

Words

by Timothy D. Holder

John 14:6 "Jesus told him, 'I am the way, the truth, and the life. No one comes to the Father except through Me.'"

When I decided to ask Jill to marry me, I gave careful thought to where I would ask her. When I showed her the ring, we hugged, and I explained to her why I picked the location I did.

My first thought was to ask her in a park where we had spent time early in our relationship. The location had sentimental value, and she loves flowers and nature. But I had decided not to do that because I thought the venue might be a little too public.

My next choice was to ask her at another location that was special. Early in our relationship, we were talking one night in my car, and I put my hand on hers and left it there. I felt it was a bold move. I would not have placed my hand on hers if I just wanted to be buddies. After what felt like a really long time, she took her free hand and put it on top of mine. That was the moment, and the location, where our relationship deepened, so I thought that might be a special place for our relationship to again deepen as we started our engagement.

When I gave Jill the ring, I held her close and launched into a whispered explanation of why I chose to give her the ring in my car. When I finally paused to take a breath, she whispered back sweetly, "You have to say the words."

She was right. I had told her many times I loved her, and I had presented her with a ring, but until I actually asked her to marry me, she couldn't really say "yes."

As Christians, we want to be a witness, but many of us struggle with being too timid to say what needs to be said. "Preach the gospel at all times and if necessary, use words." This quotation is often attributed to St. Francis of Assisi, but he never said it, and in fact it is antithetical to his theology. He preached Jesus passionately and relentlessly; he knew it was not enough to just be a nice person.

We can be nice, and we can be sweet, but niceness and sweetness won't save souls—only Jesus does that. Let us pray today for the courage to talk about Jesus with someone who needs to hear about Him. Let us be bold enough to say the words.

We need to do that today. Our someone might not have tomorrow.

Day 78

Principles

by Timothy D. Holder

Matthew 6:33 "But seek first the Kingdom of God and His righteousness, and all these things will be provided for you."

After Jill and I got engaged, we began to look for a wedding venue. We quickly found a Presbyterian Church that seemed to have the perfect look, and it was located in the perfect spot.

Let me interrupt the narrative to give some backstory. Jill has been a lifelong Southern Baptist. I was raised in the United Methodist Church. That was where I learned what it meant to be a Christian, and it was where I chose to become a follower of Christ. But I have also been a member of Southern Baptist Churches and a Christian Church. I have preached in Baptist, Methodist, and Presbyterian Churches and twice in a Wesleyan Church. I once preached at a gathering at a park that was mostly made up of African Americans whose denominational backgrounds were unknown to me. I am happy to preach to whoever will listen.

All of this is to say that I was quite comfortable in that Presbyterian Church where Jill and I thought we might get married. But then we met the pastor, and things went awry.

The pastor was a woman who told us she would need to officiate the wedding, and she would need to sit with us and talk about things beforehand. Jill told her we had already completed our premarital counseling. The pastor was actually more interested in the ceremony. She told us it would need to be inclusive, and she wanted to make sure we understood that. It was important to her that she communicate to our guests that marriage was an institution "between two people," as opposed to it being an institution between a man and a woman. She noted that most people "don't even realize it" when she slips in her inclusive references.

When Jill mentioned during our discussion where we were going to church, the pastor said, "You mean you're Baptists? *Southern* Baptists?"

It was clear from her tone that the extent of her inclusiveness did not include a group of believers who worshiped right down the street from her.

When Jill and I were alone, we decided we would look elsewhere, but the feeling was mutual. The pastor took our contact information, but she never called us.

The thing is, I agreed with this pastor's premise; I just did not share her priority. She told us she could not let us use her church to have our own service. She said she had done that once for a funeral, and the people said some things she disagreed with theologically. I respect that fact that she wanted to protect the spiritual integrity of her church. But her priority was not the Gospel; it was her definition of inclusion. At no point did she discuss the role of Jesus in our wedding, our marriage, or our lives. From everything she said during our conversation, her Good News was all about inclusiveness.

My point here is to apply this standard to us. Is our priority the Gospel, or is it something less than that—a political agenda perhaps, acceptance by a certain group of people, financial comfort, or even just the opportunity to remain within our comfort zone? Let us pray today that we would, like this pastor, take a stand on what we believe. But let us also pray today that we would take that stand on the loving and saving power of Jesus Christ.

Day 79

Everyday Miracles

by Jill Holder

Luke 12:7 "Indeed, the hairs of your head are counted. Don't be afraid; you are worth more than many sparrows."

One evening early in the summer, I went outside to the vegetable garden to plant my sunflower seeds. My parents plant lots of vegetables in the family garden that we all share. My brother's family does as well. But mostly I plant the flowers.

As I began to dig in the dirt, my eighteen-year-old son, Jackson, wandered outside with me and picked up a hoe as well. We laid rows, planted seeds, and talked together. We decided how many rows to plant, debated which type of seeds would grow the tallest, and discussed life. It was a beautiful time that warmed my heart as a mother, one of those evenings that I resolve to hold tight in my memories and pull out on a day down the road when he has moved on to college and I'm missing the sound of his laughter in the house.

It wasn't planned. It was simple. But those are the types of moments that are often the most special experiences of life.

Moments like...

When my oldest son surprised us all and came home from college just to join us in a snowball fight.

When my daughter and I picked berries together in the strawberry field in the early morning while the grass was still wet with dew.

When my middle child came running through the pasture toward me with a smile on his face.

When my youngest child sat on my lap, and we marveled at the fireworks on a July evening.

When all of my children are sitting around the dinner table, laughing and talking together.

When we eat watermelon and homemade ice cream with my parents on a summer day.

When Tim took my hand in his for the first time.

These are the times when I am reminded that God is with us in the everyday moments, the simple miracles that let us know that He is near at all times, very present and caring deeply for us.

There are many big moments in life. As I type this, Tim and I are just a few days away from our wedding, which will certainly be one of the most special events of our lives! We are very grateful for this miracle. And yet, there is an awareness that God is gifting us with beautiful moments every day that we should cherish. The challenge is to see both the big events and the daily blessings as treasures from the Lord.

Let us pray today to not miss those everyday miracles that God sends our way because of His great love for us.

Day 80

The Beginning

by Timothy D. Holder

Psalm 30:5B "Weeping may stay overnight, but there is joy in the morning."

One would think that the last entry in a devotional might be more aptly titled "The End" rather than "The Beginning," but most endings are really the beginnings of something else.

The end of school signals the beginning of summer break. The end of employment at a job marks the beginning of a new situation—either unemployment or the start of a new job.

Sometimes the end of a thing is sad, even a tragedy, and the beginning it creates is breathtakingly difficult. There are other times when the beginning of something good comes to us but only because of a great loss. Oftentimes a good thing that begins for us in such a circumstance is a closer relationship with the Lord. Maybe the Lord chooses to bless us in a way that would not have been possible without the ending of a thing that we held dear.

The point of today's message is that while it can be hard to let some things go, maybe we are being prepared for a blessing that we cannot now see.

There is a safety and comfort in that which is familiar, and some of us struggle with bitterness and frustration when we try to hold on to something that is already gone. Maybe today is the day that we have to pray for the strength to accept an end. Maybe it is time to walk toward a beginning. Let us pray for the strength to face the day.

Devotions for a New Day

Biographies

Timothy D. Holder is an author, interim preacher, public speaker, college dean, history professor, former harmonica player, and Japanese food lover. Dr. Holder's short videos can be found on YouTube, if you type in "Timothy Holder Presidents and Character." His books are usually about faith or presidents and sometimes both. Marriage to Jill has made him the happy stepfather of five and the pet owner of six.

Jill Holder is an actress, women's teacher, former children's educator, and lover of words who believes in looking for the beauty in everyday miracles. She has appeared in over 100 projects for television, commercials, and film. She is a mom of five children and lives in Knoxville, Tennessee where she enjoys life with her husband, Tim, and is passionate about teaching women to overcome difficulties and grow in a personal relationship with the Lord.

Elissa Keck Hodge is a music professor in East Tennessee who enjoys teaching college courses in music history, theory, voice, composition, and religion. Dr. Hodge and her husband, Jonathan, have three children and serve in the worship and student ministries at their local church.

Devotions for a New Day

Also by Timothy D. Holder

Presidential Trivia, 3rd edition

Devotions for the Day

Ask the Professors (Co-authored with Jason R. Edwards)

Devotions with Presidents

Presidential Stories

Presidential Character

Made in the USA
Columbia, SC
21 September 2022